UNDERSTANDING
JAMES WELCH

Understanding Contemporary American Literature
Matthew J. Bruccoli, Series Editor

Volumes on

Edward Albee • Nicholson Baker • John Barth • Donald Barthelme
The Beats • The Black Mountain Poets • Robert Bly • Raymond Carver
Chicano Literature • Contemporary American Drama
Contemporary American Horror Fiction
Contemporary American Literary Theory
Contemporary American Science Fiction • James Dickey
E. L. Doctorow • John Gardner • George Garrett • John Hawkes
Joseph Heller • Lillian Hellman • John Irving • Randall Jarrell
William Kennedy • Jack Kerouac • Ursula K. Le Guin
Denise Levertov • Bernard Malamud • Carson McCullers
W. S. Merwin • Arthur Miller • Toni Morrison's Fiction
Vladimir Nabokov • Gloria Naylor • Joyce Carol Oates • Tim O'Brien
Flannery O'Connor • Cynthia Ozick • Walker Percy
Katherine Anne Porter • Reynolds Price • Thomas Pynchon
Theodore Roethke • Philip Roth • Hubert Selby, Jr. • Mary Lee Settle
Isaac Bashevis Singer • Jane Smiley • Gary Snyder • William Stafford
Anne Tyler • Kurt Vonnegut • James Welch • Eudora Welty
Tennessee Williams • August Wilson

UNDERSTANDING
JAMES
WELCH

Ron McFarland

University of South Carolina Press

Published in Columbia, South Carolina, by the
University of South Carolina Press

Manufactured in the United State of America

04   03   02   01   00   5   4   3   2   1

Library of Congress Cataloging-in-Publication Data

McFarland, Ronald E.
  Understanding James Welch / Ron McFarland.
      p. cm. — (Understanding contemporary American literature)
    Includes bibliographical references and index.
    ISBN 1-57003-349-8
    1. Welch, James, 1940—Criticism and interpretation.
    2. Western stories—History and criticism.   3. West (U.S.)—In
    literature.   4. Indians in literature.   I. Title.   II. Series.
  PS3573.E44 Z78   2000
  813'.54—dc21   00-008544

CONTENTS

EDITOR'S PREFACE

The volumes of *Understanding Contemporary American Literature* have been planned as guides or companions for students as well as good nonacademic readers. The editor and publisher perceive a need for these volumes because much of the influential contemporary literature makes special demands. Uninitiated readers encounter difficulty in approaching works that depart from the traditional forms and techniques of prose and poetry. Literature relies on conventions, but the conventions keep evolving; new writers form their own conventions—which in time may become familiar. Put simply, UCAL provides instruction in how to read certain contemporary writers—identifying and explicating their material, themes, use of language, point of view, structures, symbolism, and responses to experience.

The word *understanding* in the titles was deliberately chosen. Many willing readers lack an adequate understanding of how contemporary literature works; that is, what the author is attempting to express and the means by which it is conveyed. Although the criticism and analysis in the series have been aimed at a level of general accessibility, these introductory volumes are meant to be applied in conjunction with the works they cover. They do not provide a substitute for the works and authors they introduce, but rather prepare the reader for more profitable literary experiences.

M. J. B.

UNDERSTANDING
JAMES WELCH

CHAPTER ONE

"My Subject Has Been Indians"
Career and Overview

When an interviewer asked James Welch in 1985 whether he considered himself an "Indian writer," he answered, "I used to be able to say that I'm an Indian who writes, and I still say that, but more and more my subject has been Indians. . . . I seem to be becoming more and more of an Indian writer."[1] In the same interview Welch, whose father is Blackfeet and mother Gros Ventre, both tribes with reservations in northern Montana, points out that he is "a breed" with "just as much Irish roots as Indian roots."[2] Born on 18 November 1940 in Browning, Montana, a town of some two thousand located east of Glacier National Park and headquarters of the Blackfeet reservation, Welch attended schools on the Blackfeet and Fort Belknap reservations. He accompanied his family to Minneapolis, where he graduated from Washburn High School in 1958, attended the University of Minnesota briefly, then worked in construction for a year before returning to Montana.

In an interview Welch described his father as a sort of "Renaissance man," who could do almost anything: "He could weld. . . . [H]e ran a TB sanitarium up in Alaska, and he's worked as an administrator of hospitals. When he retired a couple years ago he was ranching and farming."[3] On his father's side of the family, Welch is related to the white settler and trader Malcolm Clark, who took a Blackfeet wife and who was killed by a band of

Piegan Blackfeet warriors, an event that helped trigger the Marias River Massacre in 1870. Welch was to draw on that episode and on stories his father told him about his grandmother (James Welch's great grandmother), who survived the massacre, in his novel *Fools Crow* (1986). His mother, Rosella O'Bryan, grew up on the Fort Belknap reservation, home to the Gros Ventre and Assiniboine tribes, and she attended the Haskell Institute in Kansas, where she learned secretarial skills. She worked on various reservations and in Indian communities most of her adult life.

After a year at Northern Montana College in Havre, Welch transferred to the University of Montana in Missoula, where he received his bachelor's degree in liberal arts in 1965. Professor John Herrmann encouraged him to become a writer, and under the influence of Richard Hugo, who was directing the creative writing program at the time, he began to write poems and entered the MFA program, but he left without completing the degree. Poet Madeline DeFrees also aided and encouraged Welch. His first published poem appeared in a Montana poets issue of *Visions International* in 1967, and four years later, with the assistance of a grant from the National Endowment for the Arts, his collection of poems, *Riding the Earthboy 40,* was published first by World Publishing in 1971, and then in revised and expanded form as the sixth title in Harper and Row's Native American Publishing Program in 1976. He married Lois Monk, who teaches comparative literature at the University of Montana, in 1968.

Welch's poems were well received, and their appearance coincided with the publication of several important anthologies of Native American poetry, including Robert K. Dodge and Joseph B. McCullough's *Voices from Wah'kon-tah* (1974) and

Duane Niatum's *Carriers of the Dream Wheel* (1975), both of which included poems from *Riding the Earthboy 40.* Writing in the *Saturday Review,* Jascha Kessler observed that Welch's first book showed "a burgeoning talent." Welch's poems might well have gone the way of most first books of poetry, however, if it had not been for the overwhelmingly positive reception accorded his first novel, *Winter in the Blood,* in 1974. Welch worked on the second and final drafts of the novel during a year-long stay in Greece, and he received editorial advice from William Kittredge, who was teaching fiction writing at the University of Montana. *Winter in the Blood* has been described as "an almost flawless novel."[4] Both the poems and the novel have been related to what critics and scholars such as Kenneth Lincoln have described as a "Native American Renaissance" in writing prompted by the award of the Pulitzer Prize for 1968 to N. Scott Momaday's novel *House Made of Dawn.*

The critical praise of Welch's first novel was exceptional, culminating within four years of its publication in a special issue of *American Indian Quarterly* that featured half a dozen important essays devoted to it. *Winter in the Blood* is scarcely more than a novella in size (under two hundred pages in most printings), but blurbs on the cover range from Charles A. Larson's assertion from his review in the *New Republic* that it is simply "a brilliant novel" to Roger Sale's comment that it is "an unnervingly beautiful book."[5] Alan R. Velie hails the novel as "a masterpiece of comic fiction,"[6] but Welch's second novel, *The Death of Jim Loney* (1979), is, as may be inferred from the title, quite different. The novel features an apparently self-destructive and alienated half-breed, and critics have scrambled to counter charges that it is "a novel of emptiness or despair."[7] In his pamphlet on Welch for the Western Writers Series, Peter Wild concludes that it is "a badly flawed novel, not worthy of his best work."[8] More recently, however, the critical pendulum appears to have swung in favor of *Loney,* and William W. Bevis notes in an essay on Welch in *Updating the Literary West* (1997) that it is "increasingly admired by those who teach Native American literature."[9]

Between the two novels Welch produced a revised edition of his first book of poems, which won a Pacific Northwest Booksellers Award in 1975. Although he told interviewers as recently as 1985 that he intended to return to writing poems, he has not done so.[10] In 1976 Welch taught the winter and spring quarters at the University of Washington occupying the Theodore Roethke Chair, and in 1981 he began teaching there regularly during those quarters, holding a joint appointment with the departments of English and of Indian Studies. In 1981 he also received the Indian Council Fire National Achievement Award and the Montana Governor's Award in recognition of his contributions to literature. He spent the next year in San Miguel de Allende, Mexico, working on his third novel. Although he is so much "at home" in Missoula, Montana, that he could qualify as a "regional" writer, Welch often travels when he is finishing a novel. By the mid 1980s he was teaching periodically at Cornell University.

His third novel departs from his earlier work in nearly every way. *Fools Crow* (1986) is an historical novel set in the late 1860s and culminating in the Marias River Massacre and the smallpox epidemic of the winter of 1870, after which the warlike

Blackfeet made peace with the encroaching whites. *Fools Crow* is epic in scope and fictional mode, and at nearly four hundred pages, it is more than twice as long as either of his earlier novels. In commenting on Welch's poems, Peter Wild describes him as "an outside observer with an insider's understanding" of Native American experience.[11] In this novel Welch describes himself as writing "from the inside-out," unlike most historical novelists, whom he perceives as writing "from the outside looking in."[12] To create the impression of being an "insider," Welch conducted limited research into tribal lore and historical events. Describing *Fools Crow* as "an ambitious novel" in many ways, Robert Gish echoes some of the reviewers in noting its "tendency toward digression and what some might regard as a lack of tightness and coherence,"[13] but William Bevis asserts that it provides "an opportunity for us to come closer to the buffalo-culture Indian world than in any other novel to date."[14] Louis Owens concludes that the novel constitutes "the most profound act of recovery in American literature."[15] It won both a Pacific Northwest Booksellers Award and an American Book Award.

With his fourth novel, *Indian Lawyer* (1990), James Welch turned in yet another direction. Drawing on ten years of service on the Montana State Board of Pardons, he depicts a character whose life has been as successful, at least by Anglo-American standards, as Jim Loney's has been wretched. So far, however, critical response to this novel has been both slight and divided. For example, Edward Hoagland, writing in the *New York Times Book Review,* describes the novel as Welch's "most mature and readable book," and William Hoagland, writing in *Western American Literature,* observes, "The best of this very good book is its characterization."[16] Lee Lemon, however, writing in *Prairie Schooner,* argues that in this novel "the problems of being even a successful native American in our society . . . are as predictable and as unexciting as the action," and Gary Davenport, in the *Sewanee Review,* finds the characterization stalled at the level of "the 'serious' dramatic television series."[17] Davenport offers mixed praise for "the novel's metaphorical use of landscape," which only "rescues it, for the most part, from tendentiousness and banality."[18]

Welch's most recent book is an unusual thrust at nonfiction, *Killing Custer: The Battle of the Little Bighorn and the Fate of the Plains Indians,* which appeared in 1994, the same year he received the Western Literature Association's Distinguished Achievement Award and the John Dos Passos Prize for Literature. The book of essays evolved from Welch's work with Paul Stekler on the script of *Last Stand at Little Bighorn,* a motion picture made for PBS television in 1992. Like the film, which won the 1992 Spur Award from the Western Writers of America for the best television documentary script, the book is intended to "tell the Indians' side of the story" of the battle that has acquired mythic dimensions in the American psyche,[19] but as at least one historian has pointed out, Indian interpretations have received some attention over the years.[20] Presumably, however, this book is not intended for professional (or at least for "professorial") historians; certainly, Welch does not claim to possess a historiographer's credentials. The importance of this book derives from what Stella R. Swain refers to as Welch's use of the "digressive approach"; and while David N. Cremean regards the book as "rather uneven," noting that Welch "never seems entirely at home in the nonfictional world," he suggests it is "best when personal."[21] More than seventy photographs and maps add significantly to the appeal of the book.

At present Welch is finishing a novel, the title of which is *The Heartsong of Charging Elk.* Two sections from the novel were printed in the Fall 1995 issue of *Weber Studies,* but Welch's plans for it have shifted considerably since then. His original intent was to use a framing narrative involving a character named Jack Dawes, a contemporary Oglala Sioux who is a professor and who holds a doctorate from the University of California at Berkeley. He has now dropped the frame and has set the novel in France between 1889 and 1906, so it will read, like *Fools Crow,* as historical fiction. The novel centers on the life of an Oglala Sioux who, because he was ill, was left in Marseilles after Buffalo Bill's Wild West Show visited France around 1890. The show returns to France in 1905, offering the main character, who has by then acquired a French wife, the opportunity to come back to the United States.[22] This novel, which has required a couple of trips to France, will depart from other fiction by Welch in that the protagonist will not be Blackfeet. Welch, whose novels have been translated into French, among other languages, was named a Chevalier of the Ordre des Artes et des Lettres by the French cultural ministry in 1995.

If William Bevis's premise about the "homing" impulse in Native American novels needs corroboration in life, Welch's establishment of his "center" in his native Montana might serve.[23] Welch has received honorary doctorates from Rocky Mountain College in Billings (1993) and the University of Montana (1997), and he worked with William Kittredge and Annick

Smith editing the massive anthology of Montana writing *The Last Best Place,* which was published in 1988. In 1997 he received a Lifetime Achievement Award from the Native Writers Circle of the Americas.

It has become something of a critical commonplace to contextualize Welch's early career by way of political events like the takeover of Alcatraz Island in 1969 by "Indians of All Tribes" and the confrontation at Wounded Knee in 1973, which brought national attention to the American Indian Movement. Robert F. Gish, describing Welch when he spoke at the University of Northern Iowa in 1978, observes that his "strong voice and flint-honed style were much belied by his youthful, clean-cut, blue-blazer, checked-sport-shirt, horn-rim glasses look," but adds that "in his more sedate, refined way, he was as angry and rebellious as [Ray] Young Bear."[24] In speaking of the so-called "Red Power" agitation in a recent interview, however, Welch seems to distance himself from such an overtly political agenda, even as he comments on the achievements (note his use of the pronoun "they"): "I think the idea that they were radical, that they went overboard in a sense, is just what Indian people needed at that time. . . . If it weren't for AIM, I think it would be a lot harder for young people to stand up for themselves and their people."[25] Asked in 1985 whether he considered himself a "spokesman for the Indian community," Welch commented that he did not consider himself "close enough" to that community "to ever assume a role as spokesman. To be a spokesman you have to be totally involved in their community, and I'm not. . . . I'm just in my little house in Missoula, Montana, writing about Indians."[26]

Some readers and critics may be inclined to view Welch's comments as unduly modest, but questions posed by Peter Wild in his pamphlet on James Welch published more than fifteen years ago remain pertinent: "Can a person be an Indian writer when his own language is not written? And if he then must write in English, the language of the dominant culture, a foreign tongue embodying psychic, stylistic, and cultural biases, for whom shall he write?" Wild concludes that "almost all Native American fiction is written for nonIndian audiences by highly acculturated Indians."[27] In his valuable "overview" of contemporary Native American writing in all genres, published in 1996, Joseph Bruchac compares this condition to that of Africans like Wole Soyinka writing what amounts to contributions to "British literature" in using the "language of the colonizer," a circumstance that results "ironically" in "the expression of traditional values in the language of the oppressor."[28] Bruchac also touches on the vexing issue of "Who is Indian?": the issue of the *metis* or mixed-blood and the full-blood, the peculiar question as to whether the writer is "Indian enough."[29] As he points out, "Most of the contemporary generation of Native American writers have some white ancestry," and "In some cases, the white blood is proportionately equal to or greater than the Native."[30]

The issue of blood is surely exacerbated by the provocative nature of Elizabeth Cook-Lynn's essay in the Winter 1996 issue of *American Indian Quarterly,* in which she argues that "[f]or Indians in America today, real empowerment lies in First Nation ideology not in individual liberation or Americanization." That is, according to Cook-Lynn, the traditional, tribal (or communal) values are the proper concern of Native American writers, rather than indulgence in individualism (personal autonomy or self-reliance) or acceptance by the American literary mainstream, which might be regarded as an extension of the assimilation process. She insists that much of the work "done in the mixed-blood literary movement is personal, invented, appropriated, and irrelevant to First Nation status in the United States."[31] Cook-Lynn, a professor emerita at Eastern Washington University and presently editor of *Wicazo Sa Review,* asserts that "the mixed-blood literary phenomenon is not generated from the inside of tribal culture" and that "separation of these writers from indigenous communities (reservation or urban) indicates that this is a literary movement of disengagement."[32] While she mentions writers such as Gerald Vizenor, Louis Owens, Wendy Rose, Michael Dorris, Louise Erdrich, Paula Gunn Allen, and Sherman Alexie among "the major self-described mixed-blood voices of the decade,"[33] Cook-Lynn does not mention James Welch, but one would surmise that he would fit among her list of nemeses. Among the few Native American writers to emerge unscathed are N. Scott Momaday and Vine Deloria, Jr., author of *Custer Died for Your Sins* (1967). Cook-Lynn argues for a kind of story that ends not in assimilation, despair, escapism, or fantasy, but in "rebirth of native nations" and "development of worthy ideas, prophecies for a future in which we continue as tribal people who maintain the legacies of the past and a sense of optimism."[34] She argues against "poets and novelists" who are "just people who glibly use the English language to entertain us, to keep us amused and preoccupied so that we are no longer capable of making the distinction between the poet and the stand-up comedian."[35] This conservative revolutionary draws on John Gardner's text *On Moral Fiction* (1978) in grounding her sometimes reactionary views, but her perspective on what some critics must regard as a run-amok Native American Literary Bandwagon may prompt some reassessments. Specifically, Cook-Lynn assails the "bad poetry" and "bad fiction" that have been published in the aftermath of Momaday's "classic novel" *House Made of Dawn,* urging Native American writers and scholars to reflect on Gardner's warning that "bad art has a harmful effect on society" and urging "moral fiction" and "indigenous/tribally specific literary traditions" in favor of the "art for art's sake phenomenon."[36]

James Welch, as both novelist and poet, has always insisted on being taken seriously as a writer, not as an Indian who happens to write. Accordingly, while he has drawn from his own experiences as all writers do, he has assiduously avoided writing from a socioeconomic, political, or cultural agenda. It is probably significant that when Welch mentions writers who have influenced his poems or fiction, he almost never mentions Native American writers. Prior to writing his first two novels, for example, Welch had not read any of D'Arcy McNickle's fiction, even though he was a fellow Montanan whose first novel, *The Surrounded,* had appeared in 1936. (McNickle was of mixed blood and was raised on the Flathead and Kootenai reservation.) Welch's poems show no apparent influence of other important Native American poets, but no other such poet had developed anything like a reputation in the late 1960s and early 1970s, with the possible exception of Klallam poet Duane Niatum of Seattle, whose *Ascending Red Cedar Moon* was published in 1969. Welch has mentioned Ernest Hemingway's influence on his prose: "I liked his simplicity of style, his evocative style."[37] He has also pointed to Italian writer Elio Vittorini's short novel *Conversation in Sicily* as a model for *Winter in the Blood.* William Bevis points out, however, that Welch "had read McNickle and much more" before he wrote *Fools Crow.*[38] Although he spent most of his boyhood (until seventh grade) on reservations, Welch has lived away from Indian communities for most of his life, and he described himself in 1985 as having "a few Indian friends, but not many."[39] When asked how Indians have responded to his writing, Welch has consistently felt that they have "liked it, which pleases me much more than if the New York critics like my work."[40]

Perhaps because the unnamed narrator in *Winter in the Blood* speaks from the first-person viewpoint and resides in the part of Montana where Welch grew up and where his family still lives, readers sometimes assume this first novel is strongly autobiographical. In response to one interviewer, however, Welch observed, "I make up probably three-fourths of the actual situations, but maybe a fourth of them are variations of situations that I have either experienced personally or have heard of other people having experienced." He adds that "the towns are real" and that he has "never attempted to create an imaginary landscape."[41] Later in the same interview Welch declares that he is not so much interested in plot as in characters, and later still he notes that "landscape is almost the main character in anything I write."[42] Robert M. Nelson devotes a sizable chapter to Welch in his *Place and Vision: The Function of Landscape in Native American Fiction* (1993).

Moreover, Welch might be aptly described as a writer who is only secondarily concerned with ideas, if by that term one means something metaphysical or political. His interests center on the inner or psychological life of the characters, in what they are thinking and "how they're bouncing off each other."[43] His impulse to write fiction had not so much to do with a desire to make social commentary or to depict the plight of Indians in the United States today, as with the need for a "bigger canvas": "I was writing short lyrical poems and I wanted to get something, a piece of writing where I could capture the whole country and have some people in it."[44] When asked how his first novel got started, Welch told another interviewer that he "wanted to write about that Highline country in an extended way" and that when he began to consider writing prose, he "thought it was going to be a travel piece."[45] Typically, Welch establishes a protagonist in a particular time and place (the same part of Montana in his first four novels, but that will change with the novel currently in progress). He then confronts the character with a dilemma that involves his identity or sense of self (the protagonists of all four novels are men, although women do play important roles). The character struggles with the dilemma, which is more often or at least more significantly internal than external in nature, and he acquires sufficient insight or vision to make what the reader is likely to realize as a momentous decision. That decision, however, does not necessarily constitute a resolution or an effective, problem-solving response to the dilemma.

In describing his creative process with the novel, Welch has suggested that he finds the form easier than writing poems or short stories "because you can write it day by day."[46] He usually begins by trying to "think about a book for about a year, and during that year, first of all, I think about the ending. Maybe the ending won't come out the way I plan it, but I have to think that I know how it's going to end, because otherwise I'll get all balled up." After that, he thinks of "four or five high points in the novel—things that I can write toward."[47] With *Fools Crow,* he moved from writing late at night and into the small hours of the morning, as he did with the first two novels, to working in the afternoons. The most important thing in writing a novel, he notes, is that "you've got to be there virtually every day."[48] He generally writes three complete drafts of a novel before the final stage of editing.

Opening Welch's *Riding the Earthboy 40* (the title refers to a family on the Fort Belknap reservation and to the acreage) at random to a poem like "The Day the Children Took Over" or "Day to Make Up Incompletes," one would not surmise that the writer was Native American, and that could be said for as many as half of the poems in that book. On the other hand, poems like "Magic Fox," "Christmas Comes to Moccasin Flat," and "Harlem, Montana: Just off the Reservation" are indelibly Indian. The term most frequently applied to Welch's poems is "surrealistic," sometimes, as in an important essay by Alan R. Velie, modified by the word "Blackfeet."[49] Peter Wild notes in particular the "wry humor" that informs many of Welch's best poems.[50] As Wild sums it up, "a great virtue in his poetry concerning the issue of 'the Indian connection' is that he picks and chooses equally well from white society and from his Indian past to create a seamless world in which myth and reality overlap."[51]

Various critics have observed that surrealist techniques, including dreams and dreamlike disruptions of logic and reality, indulgence of the absurd, fracturing of time and chronological order, and juxtaposition of the bizarre with the ordinary are also evident in Welch's fiction, particularly in his first novel, *Winter in the Blood.* But while Welch does occasionally appropriate some elements of surrealist technique, his unnamed protagonist is most frequently described in terms that suggest a classic "existential" dilemma: the lone (isolated, alienated) individual seeking to make sense in an apparently absurd universe, where no preestablished (a priori) definitions of god, man, self, or freedom are available (hence, freedom is not a right or prerogative so much as it is a condemnation). While critics have commended Welch's comic vision in *Winter in the Blood,* the existential angst in his second novel, *The Death of Jim Loney,* attains disastrous if not tragic proportions. William Bevis, who has written of "homing" plots in Native American fiction, as opposed to plots of leaving or departure (usually to acquire more freedom or opportunity) in white or Anglo fiction, finds *Winter in the Blood* a good case in point, but *The Death of Jim Loney* more problematic. The plot of Welch's first novel appears to be circular, as the protagonist comes to terms with his past, over which he has felt a deep and alienating guilt, dissolves the "distance" between himself and others, and discovers his full-blood Indian identity. The mixed-blood Loney never goes far from Harlem, Montana, in the course of the novel, despite at least two distinct options (provided by his white girlfriend, who plans to head for Seattle, and by his sister, who lives in Washington, D.C.). But Loney's partial or vestigial awareness of his Indian heritage (whether cultural or psychic) does not seem to "save" him, as he courts his own death. Whether that death is suicidal and whether, if it is suicidal, his death constitutes a personal triumph of sorts remains a crux for many readers.

Certainly, one reason Welch's first two novels have remained in print is that they have shown the power to sustain conversation; that is, serious readers of what bookstores usually
categorize as "literature" (as opposed, for example, to "popular
fiction") find that the characters and events are worth investigat-
ing and writing about. Most critics agree that at least some
Native American context is essential in order to appreciate fully
what happens in the novels, but the extent to which readers
should feel obliged to familiarize themselves with specific tribal
(Blackfeet or Gros Ventre) lore and Indian ethnography remains
debatable. Arguably, at least an elementary understanding of
psychology (Freudian or otherwise) is also essential. Both protagonists, for example, are social misfits who are missing a par-
ent (a father in one case and a mother in the other), and both
show signs of what almost any counselor or psychoanalyst
would describe as symptoms of pathology. In fact, both protagonists struggle to maintain a grip on reality, so that one might go
so far as to suspect some form of psychosis. The point here is that
James Welch's first two novels have sustained critical conversation of a varying nature, and depending upon what experience or
perspective an individual reader brings to the texts, he or she
might read them as ethnological commentaries on the tension
between white and Indian visions or worldviews (Weltanschau-
ungen), allegories of the ongoing costs of colonialism, psychological case studies of two disturbed individuals, dramatizations
of humankind's existential crisis, or sociological analyses of
family dynamics (notably of familial dysfunction). It is this sort
of richly multiple meaning that forms the foundation of what
many readers and critics mean by "serious literature."

In his third novel Welch abandoned the contemporary setting, which featured alienated protagonists, for the world that, in
effect, shadows and haunts the lives of those characters. *Fools
Crow* directly involves both Indian (specifically Blackfeet) ethnology and Indian and white history. If one were to read Welch's
novels in an "ideal" order, it would make sense to begin with his
third, in which the protagonist (the title character) lives in a tribal
context and in harmony with his environment. Of course Welch
does not construct a Blackfeet idyll in this novel, as the tribes are
under pressure from within as well as from the encroaching
white world of the settlers, traders, and cavalry "seizers." Welch
does not pretend that to be Native American is to be, ipso facto,
morally upright, courageous, and magnanimous; in fact, he
shows painful examples of Indian adultery, cowardice, and
treachery. But as William Bevis has observed, "This is a story
about a culture where people felt whole with themselves, whole
with their past, whole with power,"[52] and the memories and remnants of that culture whisper at the edges of Welch's other novels and indeed of most other Indian fiction.

If the reader were to follow an ideal route through Welch's
novels he or she would move from the epic portrayal of the
Indian world in its last historical moment of cultural wholeness
in *Fools Crow* to the contemporary story of the unnamed Blackfeet man who recovers at least some worthwhile vestige of that
heritage in *Winter in the Blood,* and from there to the antithesis
of that character's successful survival in *The Death of Jim Loney,*
where the separation from that heritage is apparently too profound to be viable. The next novel, then, would be Welch's most
recent one to date, *Indian Lawyer,* which features a protagonist

who, like Loney, is only remotely aware of his tribal heritage, but who, unlike Loney, succeeds in the white world or the world at large. Using both his intelligence and his athletic prowess (he attended the University of Montana on a basketball scholarship), Sylvester Yellow Calf, with his law degree from Stanford, enjoys a prosperous career with a powerful law firm in Helena and finds himself being groomed for a seat in Congress. Moreover, like Jim Loney, he has a white girlfriend, but unlike Loney, Sylvester appears to be in control of the relationship. Not surprisingly, all of this "success," as measured by conventional Anglo standards, proves illusory, but the novel leaves Sylvester pretty much where the unnamed protagonist, Jim Loney, and (in a way) even Fools Crow are at the ends of Welch's other three novels: alone in the world with his integrity. (Fools Crow and his wife Red Paint are portrayed with their daughter Butterfly at the end, but by virtue of his unique vision, Fools Crow will always remain somehow apart.)

In all four of his novels, then, James Welch demonstrates the value of the native cultural heritage, and to some extent, he shows that it has healing or restorative powers. In general, he has moved from narrowly defined, rather introverted individuals toward more broadly developed, extroverted ones. Both Fools Crow, in his traditional tribal world, and Sylvester Yellow Calf, in his contemporary urban setting, interact decisively and effectively with a number of varied and at times treacherous people (characters). Much more obviously than either the unnamed protagonist or Jim Loney, Fools Crow and Sylvester make choices that impact not just their own lives, but those of others quite directly and significantly. In effect, they operate in "larger" and more complex worlds, and this is true even of Fools Crow, who lives in the tribal culture of the previous century. In this respect, at least, it must be argued that James Welch has matured as a novelist. The fact that the last two novels are each approximately twice the length of the first two may be a natural consequence of Welch's desire to probe more deeply into the lives and minds of his characters, and almost certainly the added length has contributed to the evolution of minor or supporting characters.

Undeniably, too, what might be described as the "narrative texture" of his writing has changed, and some readers will not be pleased with the results. The intensity and compression of the first two novels are not available in the latter two, and *Indian Lawyer,* perhaps because of its urban setting, hasn't the vivid landscape and power of place of *Fools Crow* (Helena, one of the smallest state capitals, has a population of about 25,000). Welch's forthcoming novel will expand to a wider arena historically and geographically as he shifts the stage to late nineteenth-century France. It will, therefore, be his first novel to take his readers outside of Montana and the first to revolve around a protagonist who is not Blackfeet or Gros Ventre (he is Oglala Sioux).

The contribution to Welch's reputation of his nonfiction *Killing Custer* is uncertain at present. Writing for the *New York Times Book Review,* Richard White observes, "Although his writing is ordinarily nuanced and subtle, he treats the intricacies of this history with a heavy-handedness that would make him wince if this were fiction."[53] In fact, this book may lie outside the purview of literary criticism, but it may prove to be of significant value for Welch himself, for it has taken him outside his "little house in Missoula" and exposed him directly to a broader world of Native American political realities. His portrayal of a meeting with Russell Means, the most widely known Indian militant of his generation, at an Elks Club outside Hardin, Montana, is surely one of the most memorable scenes in the book. Introduced as a sort of mystery guest, Means is at first "hostile and abrupt" (255), and he aims some aggressive questions at documentary filmmaker Paul Stekler, but at the end, Means joins in with the rest of them, "telling stories, laughing, teasing. He was still the center of attention, but more in the manner of a raconteur than an activist who had stirred more than one audience to action. He was Russell Means, and he could not forget that, but he gave his image a rest for this one night" (225–26). A week later, Welch reports, he heard that Means wanted to know if he would like to write his biography, but Welch did not call back, having learned that the Battle of the Little Bighorn and the Custer Myth have retained their capacity not only to generate tension between Indians and whites, but also "to create divisions among Indian people" (226).

When asked by an interviewer whether he considered characters like the unnamed protagonist of *Winter in the Blood* and Jim Loney to be "representative of Indians in general," Welch responded, "They certainly are," and he agreed that he also intended them "to typify modern Indians," especially Indian men in their twenties and thirties, when drinking sometimes becomes a problem and they reach a "crisis point" in their lives.[54] As Welch and others have observed, the disinclination to be known as an "Indian writer" at one time connected to the fear that one might be judged not as a good writer, but as a good ethnic writer/spokesman. Welch has long since joined that generation of writers who emerged in the late 1960s and early to mid 1970s as remarkably good writers (like Momaday, Leslie Silko, Simon Ortiz, and Louise Erdrich) who just happen to be Indians. The brief encounter with Means illustrates the perils of becoming a "spokesman" for any group as heterogeneous as "the Indian community," and James Welch has avoided that sort of role. Joseph Bruchac warns of the dangers of the "Who is Indian?" issue (one facet of the "Who speaks for Indians?" issue), pointing out that "there seems to be a strong bias, even now, toward discounting certain writers by saying they are not Indian enough genetically to be called Indian writers."[55] Significantly, perhaps, it is other Indian writers who are most likely to indulge that bias, and Bruchac cautions (writing just prior to the appearance of Cook-Lynn's essay in *American Indian Quarterly*), "Asserting that certain writers are not Indian because they are of mixed blood is yet another step toward total displacement and final dispossession of Native Americans." To be "seen as an Indian in the eyes of your own Native American people" is, according to Bruchac, "an excellent way to establish oneself as a Native American writer. It is also probably the best way for Native American writers to recognize themselves."[56]

CHAPTER TWO

Riding the Earthboy 40
Remaking This World

James Welch began his writing career as a poet, and although he has produced only a single volume of poems, it has been influential for various reasons, and his work appears to have secured a place for him in the presently evolving canon of Native American poetry. Moreover, what critics and reviewers have called a "poetic" or "lyrical" style has been recognized from the outset as a feature of his prose. Even after the success of his first two novels, *Winter in the Blood* and *The Death of Jim Loney,* and on the brink of the spectacular praise accorded *Fools Crow,* Welch spoke to interviewers of his intention of returning to poetry.[1] But in addition to mentioning the possibility of a series of prose poems, Welch also indicated his increasing curiosity about the experiences of urban Indians, and his next book, the novel *Indian Lawyer* (1990), was to take him in that direction. He currently has no plans to return to poetry.

Welch was brought to writing poems by the charismatic Richard (Dick) Hugo, who had himself fallen under the influence of a strong mentor when he was an undergraduate at the University of Washington: Theodore Roethke, who died in 1963. Hugo had settled at the University of Montana in 1965 after a year as a visiting lecturer in creative writing, and his thirteen-year marriage had just come to an end. For the next half dozen years Hugo led the turbulent sort of life often associated with poets like Dylan Thomas—heavy smoking and drinking, self-indulgence and remorse. When he met Ripley Schemm Hansen in the fall of 1973, most of that changed. Ripley and Dick Hugo lived on Wylie Street in Missoula, where Jim and Lois Welch still reside. In addition to writing, Hugo and Welch shared a love of one-on-one basketball and fishing (Rattlesnake Creek runs right behind Welch's house). In his introduction to Hugo's autobiography, edited by his widow, Ripley, with Lois and Jim Welch, poet William Matthews describes as a "characteristic figure" in Hugo's poems "someone who has fallen irremediably into solitude, exile and wretchedness, an emblem of pure self-pity."[2] Later Matthews notes Hugo's loyalty "to the circumstances of loss and abandonment."[3] Readers of Welch's first two novels will no doubt recognize the applicability of such terms both to the nameless protagonist of *Winter in the Blood* and to Jim Loney.

Although Alan R. Velie, Peter Wild, and Kenneth Lincoln have written perceptively of Welch's poetic technique and of the influences, no one has said much of the powerful impact of Richard Hugo, which is immediately evident in many (though by no means all) of the poems in *Riding the Earthboy 40*. (The title of the book refers to the name of a family that owned a ranch near where Welch's parents lived, and the number forty indicates the acreage of the allotment.) Instead, Velie writes of the influence of Peruvian surrealist poet Cesar Vallejo, to whom Welch was introduced by his friend and fellow poet James Wright,[4] and Lincoln suggests similarities with the poems of John Berryman.[5] Undeniably, all of these poets, like most of the well-known poets of the 1960s and 1970s, were influenced by surrealist techniques, and at times Welch seems almost "pure" in his surrealism, as in the following lines and passages (admittedly torn out of context):

Quirky grins are thick in muscatel.
Elephants are whispering in backyards.
("The Wrath of Lester Lame Bull")[6]

He turned their horses into fish,
or was it horses strung like fish
hung naked in the wind?

("Magic Fox" 3)

Velie suggests that Welch's poems generally lack the "playful humor of French surrealist verse," but they incline toward "a bitter humor and caustic wit";[7] Wild refers to it as "wry humor."[8] The examples above, however, show that Welch's humor is not always cutting, and Velie concludes that Welch "is a poet with a comic way of viewing the world" as well as "a fondness for surrealism" (as opposed, presumably, to being a surrealist per se). Both traits, Velie observes, "can be traced to his Black-feet heritage."[9]

It is just as easy, however, if not a good deal easier, to draw lines and passages from Welch's poems that hum to the tune of Hugo, who commented on the dangerously powerful influence of Theodore Roethke on himself, "probably the best poetry-writing teacher ever."[10] The danger, Hugo claims, is natural for such teachers who are also themselves good poets, partly because such poets have "obsessive ears," and they pass on their love of certain sounds (and perhaps more important, although Hugo does not mention it, of rhythms or pulses) to their students: "If he is worth a damn, any poet teaching poetry writing constantly and often without knowing it is saying to the student, 'Write the way I do.' . . . The student who shakes this, who goes on to *his* auditory obsessions and who writes the way the teacher never told him, may become a poet."[11] As Roethke was to Hugo, and to many other developing poets who came within his orbit at the University of Washington (including David Wagoner and James Wright), so Hugo was to Welch, and to many other developing poets who came under his influence at the University of Montana. Like Roethke, Hugo, "with his fierce love of kinds of verbal music, could be overly influential."[12] Arguably, some of the apparent echoes are coincidental, but in "The Only Bar in Dixon," the parallels are more than that, as both wrote on that bar and had their poems published in an issue of the *New Yorker* in October of 1970. One quatrain of Welch's poem virtually out-Hugoes Hugo:

A man could build a reputation here.
Take that redhead at the bar—
she knows we're thugs, killers
on a fishing trip with luck. (39)

The "pure" iambic pentameter of the first line is reminiscent of the fact that many of Hugo's poems are haunted by the ghost of blank verse, and the redheaded woman may very well echo the memorable one who appears in the last lines of Hugo's "Degrees of Gray in Philipsburg": "and the girl who serves your food / is slender and her red hair lights the walls" (217). Both that poem and Hugo's version of "The Only Bar in Dixon" appear in *The Lady in Kicking Horse Reservoir,* which Hugo was assembling at the time that Welch's book of poems appeared in 1971.

Both Hugo's and Welch's poems open with simple declarative sentences, and although the assertions differ considerably in nature from each other, they are similar in what one might call rhetorical mode; that is, the poems begin with a similar sort of address to the reader:

Home. Home. I knew it entering.

(Hugo)

These Indians once imitated life.

(Welch)

Hugo stays with the first person, which predominates in his poems, along with an intentionally and at times richly ambiguous use of the second person, which also figures in several of Welch's poems. As to point of view, Welch inclines more readily toward "we" than does Hugo, but the difference in the number of poems by the respective poets may diminish the significance of this observation. The important point is that in the dozen or so poems of the fifty-nine in *Riding the Earthboy 40* in which the first person plural dominates, the speaker or persona assumed by the poet is usually declaring himself as a fellow Indian. After the opening line of "The Only Bar in Dixon," the poets follow somewhat divergent paths, but their techniques of line length (free verse rhythm or pulse) and line breaks are remarkably, although not surprisingly, similar:

Green cheap plaster
    and the stores
across the street toward
    the river
failed. One Indian
    depressed
on Thunderbird.
    Another buying
Thunderbird to go.
    This air
is fat with gangsters I
    imagine
on the run. . . .
          (Hugo)
	Whatever made them
	    warm
	they called wine, song
	    or sleep,
	a lucky number on the
	    tribal roll.
	
	Now the stores have
	    gone the gray
	of this November sky.
	    Cars
	whistle by, chrome
	    wind . . .
	          (Welch)

Both poets prefer an open-ended or strongly enjambed sort of free verse line, and the tone of voice is conversational and understated, the diction and usage colloquial. The "gangsters" Hugo imagines in the seventh line of his poem emerge as "thugs" and are connected with "us" in the third quatrain of Welch's poem (cited above). At the ends of the poems, Hugo and Welch again diverge, yet they run parallel. Keyed by the phrase "no fun," Hugo has "you" reviving by heading for Hot Springs, but he echoes the word "home" five times in the last nine lines, concluding, "Five bourbons / and I'm in some other home" (212). Welch takes the phrase "no luck" and reflects on the nearby Flathead as a river that "turns away" and carries off the bodies of "Indians on their way to Canada." He then turns to "you" and offers "the redhead—yours for just a word, / a promise that the wind will warm / and all the saints come back for laughs" (39). (The "saints" in Welch's poems nearly always indicate Indians and may be an ironic reflection on the Mormons, who habitually refer to themselves as "saints," or God's elect.) While some of the parallels in these two poems obviously owe to the fact that they derive from the same site, the echoes in technique suggest something of the nature of Welch's debt to his most important teacher and close friend. It would no doubt be stretching the truth, but perhaps not exaggerating plausibility, to conjecture that part of James Welch's enthusiasm for writing poems died with his mentor in 1982.

Of course the foregoing is not to say that Welch as a poet is slavishly imitative or dependent on Richard Hugo any more than on Cesar Vallejo or James Wright. But it is to suggest that Welch was in the early stages of his development as a poet when his book appeared. Although he was thirty-one years old at the time, not an exceptionally early age for a poet's first book, Welch had been writing poems for only four or five years, and despite his early acclaim (which was not, after all, universal), one should approach his accomplishments as a poet with some perspective. Elizabeth Cook-Lynn is almost certainly not alone in thinking that especially in the immediate aftermath of Momaday's Pulitzer Prize–winning novel, *House Made of Dawn* (1968), "much bad poetry (which should be called 'doggerel') and bad fiction (which should be called 'pop art') has been published in the name of Native American art."[13] It is unfashionable and even risky for white or Anglo critics to say as much, but Robert Holland's review of *Riding the Earthboy 40* in the February 1977 issue of *Poetry* was little short of hostile, faulting Welch for an over-concern about sentimentality that drove him to sometimes "inane surrealism" and for language "not equal to the task" of saving his portrayal of the Native American dilemma from cliché.[14] Holland concludes that "Welch does little service either to poetry or to the American Indian."[15] On the other hand, Jascha Kessler, writing in an October 1971 issue of *Saturday Review,* proclaimed that Welch "shows a burgeoning talent," and he added, Welch's voice is "clear, laconic, and it projects a depth in experience of landscape, people, and history that conveys a rich complexity."[16]

Riding the Earthboy 40 consists of fifty-nine poems in four sections divided over seventy-one pages, a relatively small collection, and only about half a dozen new poems have appeared in print since the revised edition of the book was published in 1976. The poems are composed in free verse stanzas with the left margin being capitalized only where new sentences begin or where demanded by convention (for example, a proper noun). In some ways the poems could be described as "minimalist." The longest poem runs thirty-five lines, and a couple are only eight lines long; about half of the poems are under twenty lines in length. But the poems could be described as "minimalist" for reasons other than length. Kessler's depiction of the poems as "clear" and "laconic" has been echoed in various ways by such critics as Andrew Wiget, who finds them notable for "grim humor" (similar to Velie's "bitter humor," but at odds with Wild's "wry humor") and "lean picturing."[17] Joseph Bruchac suggests that the "tough, spare diction in his novels" is similar to that in Welch's poems.[18]

If one were to classify these poems, they would fall in the mainstream medium between the extremes of the New Formalist poets, whose work is celebrated in *Rebel Angels* (1996), an anthology edited by Mark Jarman and David Mason, and the Language Poets, whose work is featured in Paul Hoover's anthology, *Postmodern American Poetry* (1994). The New Formalists, including such poets as Marilyn Hacker and Dana Gioia, have been attempting, "out of need and affection" to rediscover "the inherent power of measured speech, even rhyme, and the power of narrative to convey experience."[19] The Language Poets, including such writers as Ron Silliman and Charles Bernstein, regard the poem "as an intellectual and sonic construction rather than a necessary expression of the human soul" and emphasize technique and poststructuralist linguistic theory in their work.[20] Compared with the writing of such Native American poets as Duane Niatum and Peter Blue Cloud, Welch's poems show considerably less interest in what one might call the "traditional" mode, as in the opening lines of Blue Cloud's "Sweat Lodge—The Afterwords":

Water on rocks the hiss of steam
of sage
dropped rocks into holes in space
the hissing of star-flung meteors . . .[21]

Or consider the opening lines of Duane Niatum's "The Canoe":

Fungus buried, mossy as Elwha river mist,
it is the remains of Old Man's totem.
On this earth you must breathe like the evergreens . . .[22]

Native American poets operating in this vein often focus on traditional attitudes toward nature and ritual. Sherman Alexie, following Adrian C. Louis, calls this "the corn pollen and eagle
feather school of poetry."[23]

Welch's voice is not that of the Native American tradition-
alists, and it also differs from the colloquial speech and graphic
portraits of reservation life in the poems of writers like Alexie
himself, or of Marnie Walsh's "Vickie Loans-Arrow Fort Yates,
No. Dak., 1970":

well
them white mens music
just what we like
for dancing
the floor go rockarock
I got on my red dress
my beads
tommy wear his sateen shirt
purple pink
we go round and round
push push
Saturday night whisky night.[24]

Similarly, the opening stanza of Alexie's "Futures" catches both the images and the tone of voice of reservation life:

We lived in the HUD house
for fifty bucks a month.
Those were the good times.
ANNIE GREEN SPRINGS WINE
was a dollar a bottle.
My uncles always came over
to eat stew and fry bread
to get drunk in the sweatlodge
to spit and piss in the fire.[25]

Of course few poets of any reputation speak with just a single, monolithic voice. Niatum and Alexie both have poems that could fit the category of "corn pollen and eagle feathers," and Niatum and Blue Cloud have poems that speak to the harsh realities of Indian life on and off the reservation. But the point is that Welch's poems do not comfortably fit in either of these prominent modes.

One remarkable fact that has not been mentioned about Welch's single book of poems, however, is that twenty-eight years after its initial publication, that book remains in print. Its publication history might well be interesting in its own right, as the volume has passed from World Publishing Company, where it "was not distributed and soon went out of print,"[26] only to be republished with the addition of six poems and a revised format (the original last section became the opening one) as the sixth volume in Harper and Row's Native American Publishing Program in 1976. Later still, in 1990, Confluence, a small press in Lewiston, Idaho, reprinted the Harper and Row edition, and in 1997 Carnegie-Mellon Press took over from Confluence, reprinting the book as part of its Classic Contemporaries series. Moreover, Welch's poems have maintained their status in the anthologies, starting with the inclusion of nine poems in Peter Carroll's *Young American Poets,* which appeared in 1968, three years before the publication of *Riding the Earthboy 40.* Seventeen of Welch's poems appear in Duane Niatum's influential anthology, *Carriers of the Dream Wheel* (1975), and Niatum also includes five poems in the *Harper's Anthology of 20th Century Native American Poetry* (1988). Joseph Bruchac also anthologizes five of Welch's poems in *Songs from This Earth on Turtle's Back* (1983). Welch's poems can be found in at least a dozen other poetry anthologies published since 1970.

Combining poems selected for anthologies with a list of those singled out for favorable comment and analysis by various critics over the past twenty-eight years, one can produce a fairly reliable Top Ten list (in order of the number of selections): "The Man from Washington," "Christmas Comes to Moccasin Flat," "Surviving," "Snow Country Weavers," "Magic Fox," "Harlem, Montana: Just Off the Reservation," "In My First Hard Springtime," "Grandma's Man," "In My Lifetime," "Arizona Highways." Several more poems (all anthologized at least twice) might be added to the list for various reasons: "D-Y Bar," "The Only Bar in Dixon," "Riding the Earthboy 40," "Going to Remake This World," "The Day the Children Took Over," "Never Give a Bum an Even Break." Well over half of the poems in *Riding the Earthboy 40* have been anthologized, and the first

six in the Top Ten list above each appear in at least six anthologies. While Welch's poems have a prominent place in
anthologies of Native American writing, they have also found
their way into more general collections like the *Norton Anthology of Modern Poetry* (2nd ed., 1988), Daniel Halpern's *American Poetry Anthology* (1975), and Edward Field's *Geography
of Poets* (1979).

The prevailing season of Welch's poems is winter, and if
one were to trace a key image cluster (winter/snow/ice/cold)
through the fifty-nine poems of *Riding the Earthboy 40,* at least
twenty would qualify. Moreover, the other seasons mentioned in
the poems rarely offer what one might call seasonal comforts.
"The green of spring" in "Birth on Range 18" comes "hard" (50),
and the sky is "the drab blue of spring" in "Picnic Weather,"
the last stanza of which begins, "Winter now" (12). In autumn,
which becomes less significant for being a season of bountiful
harvest than for being a harbinger of cold and snow, the reader
typically finds, as in "Surviving," a "day-long cold hard rain"
(46). In fact, considering that Montana, like much of the inland
West, is noted for dry or irrigated farming and ranching, it rains
in a surprisingly large number of Welch's poems. But as in the
poems of Richard Hugo, it is the element of wind that constitutes
so prevalent an image, figuring explicitly in about two dozen
poems, that it seems to acquire symbolic status. Elaine Jahner
describes the wind for the Blackfeet as "in every sense of the
words a 'life support system.'"[27] In "Magic Fox," the opening
poem, fish are shown to be vulnerable, "hung naked in the wind"
(3), but the wind is not so much an adversary as it is a simple fact
of life on the plains, an identifying and inescapable feature.

Jahner suggests that in poems like "Surviving," the wind "is power."[28] The mouse in "There Is a Right Way" is "part of a wind that stirs the plains" (52), and wind is "the only distance we could muster" in "Birth on Range 18" (50). The speaker in "The Versatile Historian" sees himself in autumn as "needing / wind that needed fire," and at the end of the poem, he sees himself as a "statue needing friends in wind / that needed fire, mountains to bang up against" (54). In an interview with William Bevis, Welch recalls working on the book with his editor Stanley Moss, who suggested that he had too much "wind and bones in your poems. . . . They are great symbols, but you can't keep it up forever."[29] Welch claims to have been surprised to see how often such allusions occur in his poems, and he mentions the episode as an example of "how we become used to things here that back east they might consider symbols."

In the *Handbook of Native American Literature* (1996) Kathryn Vangen comments on the four sections of *Riding the Earthboy 40* as moving "from grief and despair through anger and bitterness toward guarded hope; in the end, the cycle turns back toward grief, despair, and a sort of lame defiance."[30] In the first section, "Knives," in which four of the fifteen poems include some mention of the word "knife," she detects "images of death" presented in a sort of "elegiac quietness."[31] Velie cites the opening poem of the book, "Magic Fox," as an example of Welch's surrealism, observing that "the rules governing the poem are those of the world of dreams" and the fox is a type of "trickster figure, a being with power to transform things."[32] But Velie shies away from supplying what might be called an explication or interpretation of the poem, concluding simply that

Welch "is depicting a dream in language that is as vivid, indefi-
nite, and troubling as dreams often are."[33] It may be, however,
that the next poem in the book, "Verifying the Dead," offers
some clues as to the meaning of "Magic Fox." The latter begins,
"They shook the green leaves down" ("they" being the dreaming
men), while the former begins, "We tore the green tree down /
searching for my bones" (3, 4). The search for "my bones" is presumably the individual speaker's quest for self-knowledge (to
learn his origins), and tearing the green tree down in the process
suggests the potentially destructive nature of such analytical
ways of knowing. The fox in "Magic Fox" regards truth as "a
nightmare," and he (presumably the fox, rather than truth, although the phrasing is potentially ambiguous) turns the dream-
ers' horses into fish and ultimately into stars. "Truth," one might
argue, is merely reductive fact. The animal that appears in "Verifying the Dead" is the fox's sometime companion (and sometime adversary), a coyote (the quintessential trickster figure of
the Plains Indians). The coyote comes to drive "the day back,"
that is, to maintain night and the dream, but "we" (not "they")
kill "both him and it" (both the animal and the dream, although
"it" is ambiguous and could refer to "the day"). The result is that
"our knives" become "a bed for quick things"; that is, the per-
sonae of the poem are associated with causing death. Old Nine
Pipe confirms that the speakers have killed the coyote, which
may be associated with the imagination or intuitive (as opposed
to rational, analytic, and reductive) truth, and as "we" turn away,
"a woman blue as night" steps from the speaker's "bundle" (that
is, his medicine bundle, the repository of his personal magic),
rubs her hips (perhaps suggesting something like sensuality or

fertility) and sings "of a country like this far off." That country is the world of death, the Sand Hills in Blackfeet legend, and thus the dead are verified. The "blue woman" of "Verifying the Dead" parallels, or more accurately counters, the young girl "blonde as morning birds" of "Magic Fox." The association of the color blue with death is made clear three poems later in "Blue like Death" (9).

Such readings or explications as this run the risk of allegorizing and possibly oversimplifying the poem in the process of clarifying it, and such efforts also run the risk of misinterpretation, but poets who write in the surrealist mode tend to invite such efforts even as they seem set on resisting them. If it is valid that language is inherently ambiguous, even when those who employ it strive to be as denotative or objective as possible, it is equally valid that language inevitably communicates some manifest meaning, even when those who employ it strive to be as connotative and elusive as possible. Moreover, when a poet like James Welch mixes in poems like "Arizona Highways" or "The Only Bar in Dixon," which communicate readily even to those who do not often read poetry, he implicitly invites readers to take such interpretive risks with his more obscure or esoteric poems.

Certainly, most of the poems in the opening section of *Riding the Earthboy 40* fit Vangen's descriptive phrase, "elegiac quietness," though perhaps none fits it better than "Song for the Season" (autumn), an elegy for an unnamed man "who had done / so much" but now, "even / the trees would fold / and wither at his icy touch" (5). The ironically titled "Picnic Weather" is also elegiac: "You knew you would die some night, / alone, no folks, and I, no face, alone, / weaker in the knees and in the heart" (12).

In "Directions to the Nomad" the "noble savage," depicted as a "mad decaying creep," is the teacher of "stars," but "only to the thinnest wolf" (13). In "The World's Only Corn Palace" the sinister "they" appear again, this time armed "with knives and sticks," with which they fall upon "the wild man . . . killing all his bones" (17). The wild man may represent the poet or any person regarded as a social misfit, perhaps even a scapegoat of the corn king variety, to be sacrificed to insure a good harvest. People react to his beating by either looking away or laughing, "not loud, but blue, / a winter blue that followed / mongrels out the door." The last of the three sestets begins with an ambiguous reference: "Thunderbird came heavy on our heads." The thunderbird is a common figure in Native American myths and legends, source of thunder, lightning, and rain (hence, of fertility and life, but capable, too, of destruction), but the reference here may well be to the cheap, rotgut wine known as Thunderbird, still much in evidence among the homeless and poor of all races and ethnicities. The first-person speaker agrees with "you," who says, "Too much of a good thing / can spoil it for poets." The poem ends with the image of "us" singing "sad tunes" by the river, "and O the stars / were bright that melancholy night."

The frequently anthologized "Arizona Highways," the title of which, as has been noted by several commentators, reflects ironically on the glossy, upscale tourist magazine of the same title, features the speaker being attracted to a seventeen-year-old Navajo girl, but backing off as he sees himself "a little pale, too much / bourbon in my nose, my shoes / too clean, belly soft as hers" (19). The humorously self-deprecatory portrait here is fairly typical of the speaker's presentation of himself in the poems. While this poem does not reflect the "images of death" that Vangen finds to dominate the opening section of the book, it does end downbeat as the speaker sees his home as a "weathered nude" and as "distant." The last poem in the section, "Trestles by the Blackfoot," begins, "Fools by chance, we traveled / cavalier toward death" (21). The speaker and his friend (perhaps Richard Hugo) are fishing the Blackfoot River, which flows into the Clark Fork near Missoula, and they assume a "sentimental stance" in their bravado toward death. In the second section of the poem they spurn the "inky caps" (an edible mushroom), and the speaker playfully asks, "You see / the danger in your pose? One foot / between the ties, the other / in your mouth?" Then he returns to the inky caps for a kind of playfulness reminiscent of Theodore Roethke's poems in a childlike voice (specifically, "Dinky"): "Inky does // as inky do. It just won't do." But he promptly returns to perilous reality: "Funky jokes can't separate / this monster from his meal." Presumably, the "monster" is death, and as soon as he has uttered the warning, the speaker employs a phrase familiar to readers of Hugo's poems, "Let's be nice." He invites his friend to pretend they are cats returning from a night on the town, "knives between / their teeth," as if they were (to double up the metaphor) boys pretending to be cats playing pirates. Then he returns to the fish (as in the first poem of this section), now cleaned, "sliced and faded."

Vangen finds the tone shifting "toward anger and bitterness" in the second section of *Riding the Earthboy 40,* as it "moves into historical portrayal," but despite the anger and despair, she observes that the "poems contain an underpinning of grief and compassion."[34] The title of the section, "The Renegade Wants

Words," suggests a pun, whereby the renegade (a loaded word when it comes to Indian affairs) both desires and lacks the words or language to express his anger and confusion; that is, the reader may see these poems as yearnings, or as expressions of loss. Obviously, the two conditions are not mutually exclusive. The sixteen poems in this section concern "history" primarily in the sense of "current events." Five of the poems are among the list of the ten most frequently anthologized (and four are from the list of six additional poems indicated above), a fact that suggests that this section represents Welch at his best as a poet.

The opening poem of the section, "In My First Hard Springtime," is among the first that Welch submitted to Hugo when he took a creative writing class from him in 1967:[35]

> Those red men you offended were my brothers.
> Town drinkers, Buckles Pipe, Star Boy,
> Billy Fox, were blood to bison. Albert Heavy Runner
> was never civic. You are white and common. (25)

Hugo is supposed to have said that by the time he finished this opening quatrain, he knew he "had nothing to teach this young man except to tell him to keep writing."[36] The next poem, "Christmas Comes to Moccasin Flat," confronts the reader with the reservation world of poverty in which the "wise men" must purchase their candles on credit because the price for calves has fallen and friends stare out plastic-covered windows as they wait for commodity food. Charlie Blackbird is located equidistant (twenty miles) from two major forces of acculturation, "church and bar," trying to start a fire with flint. His counter-

part, the more traditional Indian, Medicine Woman, is connected with "clay pipe and twist tobacco" and can call "each
blizzard by name," but she is also locked in conflict with time,
predicting "five o'clock by spitting at her television" (26).
Children beg her for a traditional story in which warriors will
bring food in the context of "a peculiar evening star, quick
vision of birth." But Welch does not allow the poem to end quietly there. Instead, he returns tersely to Charlie, punning on the
word "quick" (both "alive" and "rapid"): "Blackbird feeds his
fire. Outside, a quick 30 below."

Although there are surreal moments among the poems in this
section (a line here, a metaphor there), the mimetic mode predominates. The persona depicted in the third poem, "In My Lifetime," is "the wrong man, a saint unable / to love a weasel way"
(27). The term "saint" appears to be synonymous with "Indian"
(as suggested above), but this man's inability to love "a weasel
way" (that is, cunningly) makes him "wrong." Later in the poem
he is said to be sinful and is described as a "fool." Presumably, a
man who loved in a cunning manner would be "right" because he
would be clever, and implicitly that is what it takes to survive in
this world. Yet it is clear that this "wrong man" is actually "right."
He drinks "the wind that makes the others go," and he runs "the
sacred way" (the "others" are the "children of Speakthunder," or
Thunder, the powerful god connected with the origin of the
Blackfeet medicine pipe);[37] that is, he is in sync with the natural
world, which is why he can "chase the antelope naked / till it
drops." In the second section of the three-part poem, we are told
that this "fool" is now dead, but presumably there are "signs that
say a man could love his fate," even though in this case that fate,

"winter in the blood," is "one sad thing." In the ironic mode of this poem, it follows that if this saint is not truly "wrong," then he is not truly a "fool." It is from this passage that Welch took the title of his first novel, and the persona in this poem may provide something of a gloss on the novel, or at least one key to its unnamed protagonist. In the last section the speaker enters the poem himself, refusing to "explain" the wrong man's sins and desperately undertaking the wrong man's destiny. Like the character in the poem, the speaker undertakes to "run these woman hills, translate wind / to mean a kind of life," for he now realizes that "the children of Speakthunder / are never wrong." This is not so much a contradiction of his initial assertion in the poem as it is a correction: only the "wrong" man (who must suffer considerably in the world because he will love honestly, not stealthily or shrewdly) is "right." The speaker's conclusion indicates that he, too, is in sync: "I am rhythm to strong medicine." Welch moves by way of a triple rhyme in the last four lines of the poem from "my song," to "never wrong," to "strong medicine." This poem may very well be a sort of *ars poetica,* for it could be argued that translating wind is exactly what poets do.

"Harlem, Montana: Just off the Reservation," although it is separated from "In My Lifetime" by two other poems, reads as if intended to follow it directly, as it opens, "We need no runners here" (30). In the two intervening poems the speaker laments "our past is ritual" ("Spring for All Seasons" 28) and depicts an Indian named Deafy whose ears the wind has shut "for good" (the pun is almost certainly intentional) and who dreams "of a moon, the quiet nights and a not quite done / love with a lady high in costly red shoes" ("There Are Silent Legends" 29). In other words, both of

the intervening poems draw images from "In My Lifetime." But
the progress of the poems is toward a cynical humor that comes off
most effectively in "Harlem, Montana," which is also the longest
poem in the book at thirty-five lines. (Harlem, a town of about one
thousand, is located just north of the Fort Belknap reservation in
north central Montana, an area known as the Highline, and the
town reappears in Welch's novels.) In this town "Booze is law /
and all the Indians drink in the best tavern. / Money is free if
you're poor enough." The constable is "a local farmer" who
"plants the jail with wild / raven-haired stiffs." In the second section the speaker says good-bye to "Harlem on the rocks," as if it
were a sort of whiskey, "so bigoted, you forget the latest joke."
Here, Welch becomes about as strident in his political voice as he
gets, declaring that the whites of Harlem would "welcome a bat-
talion of Turks / to rule your women," even though "Turks aren't
white. Turks are olive, unwelcome / alive in any town." (The fact
that most Turks regard themselves as more European than Asian
is not necessarily relevant here.) The third section of the poem
opens with an echo of Hugo:

> Here we are when men were nice. This photo, hung
> in the New England Hotel lobby, shows them nicer
> than pie, agreeable to the warring bands of redskins
> who demanded protection money for the price of food.
> Now, only Hutterites out north are nice. We hate
> them. They are tough and their crops are always good. (30–31)

Curiously, the "we" at this stage of the poem becomes the prej-
udiced Anglos, who are no more tolerant of the German immi-

grant Hutterite farmers than they are of "redskins." The "protection money for the price of food" demanded by the Indians is simply that which was promised them in their treaties. The poem ends with a scolding of Harlem for its hypocritical hatred of "the wild who bring you money," followed by a comical reminiscence of "three young bucks who shot the grocery up, / locked themselves in and cried for days, we're rich, / help us, oh God, we're rich." Or is the memory simmering with sarcasm, and therefore not so much comic as it is bitter? If the reader accepts the last lines as comical, then they provide a sort of relief for what threatens at times to turn into a polemic. But if the humor of the closing lines strikes the reader as sarcastic, then the anger of the poem is sustained.

After the emotional energy of "Harlem, Montana," the title poem of the volume, which follows, seems almost anticlimactic. Earthboy is described as "simple" and he wears a hat said to be "clowny." Like the poet, he farms both land and sky "with words" (32). The word that reverberates throughout is "dirt," and the poem ends quietly, "Dirt is where the dreams must end." The first-person speaker in the next poem, "Going to Remake This World," turns away almost completely from the mode of denunciation that threatens to turn "Harlem, Montana" into diatribe. As snow falls in the morning, he watches "Indians / on their way to the tribal office"; then, as if aware of the flatness of the previous image, Welch writes, "Grateful trees tickle the busy underside / of our snow-fat sky" (33). Readers will have to decide for themselves whether this startling, playful image amounts to a welcome disruption of the mundane routine, or is a gratuitous imposition on the otherwise understated details of the poem. Immediately, the speaker reflects, "My mind is right," perhaps echoing a passage in "Skunk Hour," one of Robert Lowell's best known poems, "My mind's not right."[38] The speaker, who is apparently but not certainly white ("remaking" the world sounds suspiciously like the ambition of an Anglo), is awaiting someone, most likely a woman. When he sees Doris Horseman and her "raving son" Horace who "doesn't know," the reader may not initially connect her with her waiting lover, but when the boy kicks the speaker's dog and "glares at me," Welch ascribes to the speaker an attitude reflecting that of the whites of Harlem: "too dumb to thank the men / who keep him on relief and his mama drunk" (of course it could be argued that the "men" here are not necessarily whites). Then the speaker is reminded of the outside world, Hawaii calling at two o'clock, the weather report from Moose Jaw, Saskatchewan, and he reflects, "Some people . . . ," but does not finish the thought. He ends with a plea, "if you do not come this day, today / of all days, there is another time" when the weather is pleasant: "Sometimes, / you know, the snow never falls forever." Welch teases the reader here with an implied oxymoron, playing "sometimes" against "forever."

The thirteen lines of "The Man from Washington," which is probably Welch's best-known poem, reflect upon the type (or stereotype) of "those who matter." Here, the "we" in the poem is clearly the Indians who "didn't expect much more / than firewood and buffalo robes / to keep us warm" (35). The "man" (in the street slang sense of the word) is depicted as "a slouching dwarf with rainwater eyes" who promises that life will go on "as usual" and everyone will be "inoculated / against a world in which we had no part, / a world of money, promise and disease."

This poem is certainly Welch's most directly political statement, but it is not as representative of his best poems as the next one in the book, "Blackfeet, Blood and Piegan Hunters" (the title refers to the three tribes that make up the Blackfeet nation). In this poem, as in several others, Welch uses repetition of key words for rhetorical impact. In the opening stanza, for example, he repeats morphemes of "end" three times in the first four lines (the rhetorical term for this is "polyptoton"):

> If we raced a century over hills
> that ended years before, people couldn't
> say our run was simply poverty or promise
> for a better end. We ended sometime
> back in recollections of glory, myths
> that meant the hunters meant a lot
> to starving wives and bad painters. (36)

The repetition of "meant" in the sixth line continues the rhetorical play, and the words "glory," "myths," and "hunters" are repeated in the next stanza, in which children "need a myth that tells them . . . / forget the hair that made you Blood, the blood / the buffalo left" (the capitalized "Blood" indicates the Blackfeet tribe, also known as "Kainah"). The word "buffalo" is then echoed in the third stanza, where a morpheme of "mean" appears in the line, "Meaning gone, we dance for pennies now." In the last four lines of the poem the word "look" appears three times:

> . . . Look away and we are gone.
> Look back. Tracks are there, a little faint,

our song strong enough for headstrong hunters
who look ahead to one more kill.

The rhetorical device of repetition subtly emphasizes the transition from "meaning" being "gone" to "we" being "gone" altogether. The word "hunters" has now appeared in all three stanzas, and Welch also puns on strong/headstrong and headstrong/ahead in these lines. Internal rhyming abounds as the poem ends: back/tracks, song/strong/headstrong.

In the last two sections of *Riding the Earthboy 40,* the first of which is titled "Day after Chasing Porcupines," Vangen detects a "philosophical tone . . . of guarded hope."[39] This section, which consists of ten poems, includes two of Welch's most frequently anthologized and commented upon, "Surviving" and "Snow Country Weavers." In the former, during a cold day in late fall the Indians huddle "close as cows before the bellied stove" and tell stories. Blackbird, who is most likely Charlie Blackbird from "Christmas Comes to Moccasin Flat," says, "Oftentimes, when sun was easy in my bones, / I dreamed of ways to make this land" (46). He chooses the word "make," rather than "remake," which is the term used by the white speaker in "Going to Remake This World." Blackbird's story is broken by references to other birds: "We envied eagles easy in their range"; "Sparrows skittered through the black brush." That night "wet black things" steal their cache of meat; however, the speaker does not complain, but simply states in the last line, "To stay alive this way, it's hard. . . ." In "Snow Country Weavers," a spare poem of just twelve lines, the speaker begins by informing us that "things are well" (47), but typically, he is satisfied with minimal signs of well-being: "Birds flew south a year ago. / One returned, a blue-winged teal / wild with news of his mother's love." As duck hunters know, the teal is among the smallest ducks, so the speaker's optimism is guarded to say the least. In the second stanza he tells us ("you") that "wolves are dying at my door," which indicates that the winter is indeed harsh. In the last quatrain the speaker says he "saw your spiders weaving threads / to bandage up the day," but these spiders are more than symbols of healing, for "those webs were filled with words / that tumbled meaning into wind." The spiders, then, behave like poets, providing meaning for the incessant element that blows through the world Welch depicts.

In "The Versatile Historian," the last poem of the third section, the first-person speaker portrays himself as a singer/poet in autumn, but initially it is unclear whether the speaker or the forests are "needing / wind that needed fire" (54). The sun tells him to "forget / the friends I needed years ago." The sky and the "chanting clouds" that "crowded against the lowest peak" are all he needs to sing about "trouble to the north," but "Sleeping weasels robbed / my song of real words. Everywhere, rhythm raged." Now the sun that was overhead, in the trees, earlier in the poem appears beneath the speaker's feet, and he becomes "the statue needing friends in wind / that needed fire, mountains to bang against." In effect, the poem expresses the interdependence or mutual need of everything in the world.

The last dozen poems in *Riding the Earthboy 40* are gathered in a section titled "The Day the Children Took Over," and the title poem opens ambiguously: "And though the sky was bright, snow fell down. / Children ran out. Mothers read letters / that said the world would end in fire" (57). Of course no such apocalyptic fire is likely to burn while snow is falling, and this snow is associated with "lovers locked together / in bedrooms." But it also falls "with a vengeance" on politicians and on "Priests who left the pulpit for a fine new wife / walked about, pure and heavy beneath a wet sun." Welch playfully puts an end to clerical celibacy here, but the children have the last word in the poem as they run out and play in the snow and build snowmen, creating "life, in their own image." Not all of the poems in the last section are as upbeat as "The Day the Children Took Over." The next poem, "Call to Arms," seems to speak to the political issues of the late 1960s: "We spoke like public saints / to the people assembled in the square" (58). But the speeches and gestures succeed only in bathing the town "in public guilt," and the playful children of the previous poem become "whiny kids" that break loose and charge the field "armed with sticks." In the third quatrain Welch offers an oxymoron that suggests the confusion, as men weep and women "beat the savage mildness / from their hearts." In a risky pun, Welch then proclaims, "The eyes were with us, / every one, and we were with the storm." As the "public saints" ride out into the storm that night, "None looked behind, / but heard the mindless suck of savage booted feet." If this reading of the poem is accurate (the text remains open to discussion, of course), Welch is indicating here some reservations about the efficacy of strident political protests, even by those who can speak like saints.

"Grandma's Man," one of Welch's almost linear narrative poems, has been praised for its humor. Here the grandmother must deal with two fools, the "silly goose" that bites the hand that has fed it and her foolish husband, who neglects his farm to

become an artist. The goose is now "preening in her favorite pil-
low," but her husband proves a greater challenge (64). His effort
to paint the episode of the goose that bit his wife's hand fails, but
"In wind, / the rain, the superlative night, images came, geese /
skimming to the reservoir. This old man listened." The grandfather presumably remains a mediocre painter, but as Velie
observes, even bad painters "look more closely at familiar things
than do other people, and consequently see much more than non-
painters."[40] This painter becomes most adept when the sky turns
white and he can paint snowflakes, but "He never ever / got
things quite right. He thought a lot about the day / the goose bit
Grandma's hand. LIFE seldom came / the shade he wanted"
(65). Velie sees the old painter in the role of the "wise fool," like
Don Quixote, while Peter Wild suggests that Welch is offering a
tongue-in-cheek "homily on the condition of himself and all
artists" with respect to the "smug and unappreciative world."[41] In
the last lines of the poem Welch puns on the word "well": "Well,
and yes, he died well, / but you should have seen how well his
friends took it." The humor here is very broad.

Most poets are hyperconscious of the poems they select to
open and close their books, and James Welch almost certainly
gave considerable thought to his decision to end with one of his
most upbeat lyrics, "Never Give a Bum an Even Break," a title
that looks back to the W. C. Fields film *Never Give a Sucker an
Even Break* (1941), which was one of Richard Hugo's favorites.
The bum in this poem is one who "could have come to tell us /
of his new-found luck—the strolling / players who offered him a
role / in their latest comedy" (71). But instead he has come to
speak "of a role so black the uncle died / out of luck in a west-

end shack." (It is tempting to identify the "he" of this poem with Hugo, which would account for the solicitude shown by the speaker as he walks the man to the door and sits down with him "under one of the oldest bridges in town," but such an identification would not necessarily enhance the impact of the poem.) The reason Welch selected this poem to conclude the book most likely has to do with its final lines: "Any day we will crawl out to settle / old scores or create new roles, our masks / glittering in comic rain." Peter Wild connects these masks with Indian "ceremonial masks" that have "lost their power."[42] but while that reading is attractive, it seems just as likely that Welch is using the term more broadly to indicate the universal tendency of people to create their own identity and in particular to assume whatever mask they think appropriate for the occasion. Certainly, the image of the masks "glittering in comic rain" leaves the reader with a cheerful impression that he or she is at one with the poet, part of the "steady demolition team" that can tear down old structures, crawl out from under the debris, take care of past problems, and create afresh. There is also in that image what might be called a "promise," on Welch's part, of things to come. As Kenneth Lincoln observes of the last section, "These closing poems register a spirit of reconciliation and defiant reaffirmation."[43]

CHAPTER THREE

Winter in the Blood as American Picaresque Classic

One could write a sizable essay on the thriving critical industry that has grown up around James Welch's first novel, *Winter in the Blood,* which he wrote between 1971 and 1973. The novel was published in 1974, five years after N. Scott Momaday won the Pulitzer Prize for fiction and opened up the literary frontier for Indian writers. Welch has reflected on what he thinks the novel is about and on the unnamed protagonist, who continues to intrigue readers and to spur an array of interpretations that are sometimes dazzling in their ingenuity. Stephen Tatum's essay on the novel, for example, is perceptive and thought-provoking, despite the heavy cargo of current critical jargon: "*Winter in the Blood* critiques any optimistic faith in the privatized consciousness's ability to construct a redemptive space safe from the inscription of the dominant culture's ideology."[1] Readers who encounter the many critical responses to this novel may agree that finding the "right" interpretation of the characters and events is not so important as coming to terms with the text on their own and coming to an understanding of it that is both sensible and satisfying.

Winter in the Blood was published twenty-five years ago, and its critical reception was almost unanimously positive; the Viking Penguin reprint of 1987 heralds the novel as "The Classic Tale of Indian Life Today." Literary scholars in recent years have sometimes preferred the term "privileged text" to describe such works. The term suggests immunity from adverse or negative criticism, and it has been applied to such works as Hawthorne's *The Scarlet Letter,* Twain's *Huckleberry Finn,* and Hemingway's *The Sun Also Rises.* While *Winter in the Blood* may be at some distance yet from that neighborhood, it is headed in the right direction, and it is well established in the canon of Native American literature. Such texts acquire their status these days by attracting and sustaining the interest of literary scholars as expressed, typically, in two ways: first, by being adopted as texts for the classroom; second, by prompting serious critical inquiry as expressed in essays and articles in scholarly journals and in books. As one writer on this novel observes, an important part of justifying the use of a novel like *Winter in the Blood* in the classroom is to establish its "intrinsic worth" as "literary art" and to demonstrate that the novel "contains all the complexity and richness of great literature."[2] One measure of this novel's popularity in the classroom is that already at least twenty master's theses and doctoral dissertations have been written on it, sometimes by itself, other times in the context of other works, like Ivan Doig's *English Creek,* which is also set in Montana, or novels by other Native American writers, like Leslie Silko, D'Arcy McNickle, and N. Scott Momaday.

For contemporary writers in the United States this kind of attention usually begins with stellar reviews written by well-established critics for such periodicals as the *New York Times Book Review.* No American author could hope for a warmer welcome than Welch received for his first novel. Reynolds

Price filled the front page of the *New York Times Book Review,* insisting that it is "by no means an 'Indian novel.' . . . What it is is a nearly flawless novel about human life." He also praised its "young crusty dignity, its grand bare lines, its comedy and mystery, its clean pathfinding to the center of hearts."[3] Roger Sale, writing for the influential *New York Review of Books,* preferred *Winter in the Blood* to the other three novels he was reviewing and commended Welch for "constantly fending off easy attitudes and conclusions with a flat, brooding precision"; he went on to proclaim it "an unnervingly beautiful book."[4] Noting the rather slender plot of the novel, Sale praised Welch's "instinct" on that score to be "just right."[5] Charles R. Larson, who was to return to the novel four years later in his book *American Indian Fiction,* concluded that it was "a beautiful book, put together with loving care . . . a work of perfect unity and finish. For some readers this will be the most significant piece of Indian writing they have yet encountered; for others, it will be simply a brilliant novel."[6] Larson drew particular attention to the tone of "elegiac quietness" and the "impressive" use of humor.[7] The editorial decision of the *New Yorker* that demoted the novel to the "Briefly Noted" section of the review column was almost singular in describing it as an "interesting, if seriously flawed, first novel," complaining that "there is too much that is simply callow and unappealing about the character, and though the author's observations about nature are almost always satisfying, his portraits of the other characters are frustrating."[8] Margo Jefferson in *Newsweek,* however, described the novel as "beautiful and austere" and suggested that its power "lies in the individual scenes, with their spare dialogue and piercing detail."[9] In the two and a half decades that have followed these rave reviews, *Winter in the Blood* has become a staple in many college and university classrooms, and it has generated more than fifty scholarly essays or chapters of books, including a special issue of *American Indian Quarterly* that appeared four years after the novel was published.

Thanks to such interviewers as William (Bill) Bevis and Nicholas O'Connell, quite a bit is known about Welch's intentions with the novel and about his process of composing it. For example, the novel is narrated from the first-person perspective of an unnamed protagonist who does not appear to have much in common with the author except his age, his Blackfeet heritage, and perhaps a fondness for fishing and small-town bars: "The bars I write about are bars I have known and can envision in my mind."[10] Although William W. Thackery has been at some pains to demonstrate the importance of age thirty-two in the age-graded societies of Gros Ventre men, it is perhaps just as likely that the unnamed protagonist of the novel is thirty-two because that is the age Welch happens to have been as he worked on the final drafts of it in 1973. The interview with O'Connell indicates that Welch bases his fiction on "real people, real landscapes, real situations," and of course the section of northern Montana described in *Winter in the Blood* was where he grew up and where members of his family still live. In fact, he goes so far as to observe in that interview that "landscape is almost the main character in anything I write,"[11] and he tells O'Connell that when he wrote his first novel he "wanted to write about that Highline country in an extended way, and my poems just weren't doing it. . . . When I first started thinking about a piece of prose writing, I thought it was going to be a travel piece."[12] In an earlier interview Welch told William Bevis that he "knew right out this was not going to be a heavily plotted novel,"[13] but his comments to O'Connell suggest that place or setting came not only before plot, but even before character when he began his work on the novel. This may explain why some readers have a hard time following the plot, even though they find the character engaging or at least sympathetic in some ways, and even though the many episodes seem vivid and powerful.

Interviews also tell something of Welch's writing process with this novel: "When I wrote *Winter in the Blood,* I wrote the second and third drafts in Greece. And I would spend from about ten o'clock at night 'til two in the morning writing."[14] Welch told Bevis that the novel went through four drafts before he sent it to Ted Solotaroff, his editor at Harper and Row, and before that, all he knew was that his wife Lois and eventual Pulitzer Prize– winning poet James Tate "liked it a lot."[15] Welch does not hesitate to credit University of Montana professor of creative writing William Kittredge for his rigorous editing of the first draft: "Man, he went through with a red pencil. Every page was mark- ed up—it was a terrific reading job. But it was also very heart- breaking, because I thought at least it would be readable and tell a story and approximate a novel."[16] Welch's reaction to his friend's critique, after the initial shock, was to sit down with him and work through the manuscript in an all-night session: "We went through it page by page and he showed me where I had messed up."[17] Welch credits Kittredge for teaching him "things like dialogue. . . . My beginning dialogues were very wooden, people speaking directly to each other back and forth. Kittredge taught me a simple little trick, that people talk over each other's shoulders."[18] Welch pays a tribute of sorts to his friend by naming the Catholic priest in his novel "Father Kittredge."[19]

Welch has told interviewers that the "structure" of his first novel was patterned on that of Italian writer Elio Vittorini's novel *Conversazione in Sicilia:* "Nothing much happens in the book, just incidents and situations, discoveries and so on. And in a sense, nothing much happens in *Winter in the Blood.*"[20] Oddly, given the passion of literary scholars for textual allusions and source studies, this lead has been followed only by A. LaVonne Ruoff, who focuses on parallels among the characters and use of dialogue, observing, for example, that the mothers in both novels are "formidable, practical women who hold their romantic husbands in considerable contempt."[21] Even a cursory glance at Vittorini's novel, however, suggests various other kinds of influence. Although his writing has not been widely read in the United States, Elio Vittorini (1908–66), is respected in Europe for his novels and nonfiction, and Italo Calvino described *Conversazione in Sicilia* (1941; serialized between 1938 and 1939), Vittorini's best-known novel, as "the manifesto and the basis of modern Italian literature."[22] A close examination of Vittorini's novel, translated as *In Sicily* and published in 1949 by New Directions, would suggest any number of parallels, but some of them would be coincidental and of little direct relevance. For example, the age of Silvestro, Vittorini's first-person protagonist, is almost thirty, a point which, some might argue, gives him something in common with Welch's main character, and each of the men has a brother who has died violently—Silvestro's in combat during World War I. In a brief introduction to the novel Ernest Hemingway draws attention to Vittorini's bringing of metaphorical rain to the literary desert, and he encourages readers to overlook any "rhetoric or fancy writing" that might annoy them: "Remember he wrote the book in 1937 under Fascism and he had to wrap it in a fancy package."[23] While Vittorini's style is not likely to strike most readers as at all florid, Hemingway, who was Welch's favorite novelist at the time he was writing his own first novel, had offered an added warning against stylistic excess. An admirer of straightforward realist prose, Welch mentions John Steinbeck as another important writer to him.[24]

If other literary scholars have consulted Vittorini's novel, they have most likely found that Welch's hasn't a great deal in common with it, but at least two observations are worth making. First, the psychological or spiritual condition of Silvestro when the novel begins is reminiscent of the "distance" that separates Welch's protagonist from his family (most notably his mother, Teresa) and friends: "That winter I was haunted by abstract furies. I won't try and describe them, because they're not what I intend to write about. But I must mention that they were abstract furies concerning the doomed human race. They had obsessed me for a long time, and I was despondent. . . . My life was like a blank dream, a quiet hopelessness."[25] One obvious and important difference between Vittorini's protagonist, who speaks here, and Welch's is that the latter lacks the kind of perspective or self-awareness that one encounters with a writer, but the narrators do share a sense of alienation for which winter appears to be the apt seasonal symbol. When a twenty-page excerpt from his novel in progress was published in the *South Dakota Review* in the summer of 1971, the editors quoted Welch's description of it as a novel "about an Indian man in his early thirties who is *haunted by abstract furies* and the emptiness of his relations with other people" (italics inserted).[26] Welch's novel begins with a much more vivid and less abstract scene, and the fact that his narrator (also a first-person protagonist) is not a writer, as is Vittorini's, may account for his inability to conceptualize his dilemma in words, despite the fact that he is sharply aware of the physical details of his surroundings: "In the tall weeds of the borrow pit, I took a leak and watched the sorrel mare, her colt beside her, walk through burnt grass to the shady side of the log-and-mud cabin. It was called the Earthboy place, although no one by that name (or any other) had lived in it for twenty years" (1). In place of phrases like "haunted by abstract furies" and "doomed human race," Welch offers "tall weeds of the borrow pit," a mare and her colt, "burnt grass," and "the shady side" of a "log-and-mud cabin." In his opening paragraph Welch refers to the caved-in roof of the cabin as "a bare gray skeleton, home only to mice and insects"; to "tumbleweed, stark as bone" lodged by the "hot wind" against the cabin wall; and to "a rectangle of barbed wire" that encloses "the graves of all the Earthboys" except for a daughter "who could be anywhere."

As Welch puts it in one interview, he found a novel written by a poet, which is what he was himself at the time, and it taught him that one did not have to have the "whole sweep" of a meticulously plotted novel in mind, but "could work from scene to scene."[27] Both novels feature a great deal of dialogue, although it is a much more prominent element in Vittorini's, which suggests both that his novel has more of a dramatic texture (and presumably that his protagonist is more communicative) and that Welch's offers more narrative of events and more self-reflection on the part of the main character. This sort of narrative structure also invites quick and abrupt transitions in scene and multiplicity of distinct episodes. Its advantage is rapidity of pace, and its drawback is a tendency toward elision or compression of details, which some readers of more conventionally constructed novels might find confusing, but such sudden transitions and missing details are a common feature of surrealism, which is another technique that Welch sees himself as having emulated.[28]

Welch constructs this highly episodic novel in four parts and an epilogue, but he creates a curious structural imbalance in the process, as a hasty "quantitative analysis" will illustrate. Part 1 consists of seventeen "sections" (it would not be accurate to call these "chapters" in any conventional sense, as the lengthiest run only about seven pages, and section 6 amounts to little more than a brief paragraph); these cover some sixty pages, so a typical section runs just three or four pages. The second part of the novel is constructed similarly (about sixty-four pages distributed over fourteen sections). But the third and fourth parts are much condensed: part 3 consists of just six sections and about twenty pages, while part 4 is composed of twenty-three pages set up in five sections. The epilogue runs about three pages. What this kind of organization provides is a very rapid, almost hectic pace and an opportunity for frequent, abrupt transitions. A part-by-part summary will illustrate how this structure works.

Part 1 opens with the narrator returning home from a barroom altercation with a white man, only to find that Agnes, his Cree girlfriend, has left, taking his .30–30 and his electric razor.

WINTER IN THE BLOOD

Most of the interpretive angles into the novel are implicit in the first half dozen pages. The emotional or psychological "distance" of the narrator, which is reflected in the deserted Earthboy ranch and the huge emptiness of the Milk River country on the Montana Highline, sets up the major dilemma to be dealt with (or "resolved"—critical perspectives vary on that issue). Readers who emphasize the importance of Native American history and ethnography have been quick to point to the traditional animosity between the Blackfeet and the Cree, implicit in the narrator's grandmother's dream of killing the girlfriend. Readers who incline toward conventional (some would say Eurocentric) symbols and myths have observed that Agnes, whose name suggests an ironic connection to *agnus dei* ("lamb of God"), attempts to emasculate the narrator by taking items that are symbolic of his manhood.

The transitions between sections are often abrupt and without logical or causal connection. In addition to emphasizing the fractured nature of the protagonist's experiences, this leaping over logic or causality deals with time, as Welch points out in an interview, in a similar manner to that in his poems, where he tries to create "the sense of keeping the poem moving, keeping it jumping, don't dwell too much on transitions, that kind of thing."[29] For instance, the second section ends with the grandmother plotting ways to slit the Cree girl's throat: "the paring knife grew heavy in the old lady's eyes" (5). The opening sentence of the next section is, "I slid down the riverbank behind the house" (5). Readers will be either attracted or confused by such sudden leaps, but they will encounter many by the end of the novel. Welch abruptly locates the narrator at the river, fishing without success, which is not surprising, as the narrator is well aware that the Milk River sustains no fish population, despite the efforts of the fish and game department to stock it. Readers familiar with the myth of the Fisher King, which underlies T. S. Eliot's *The Waste Land,* have speculated that the narrator is connected somehow with the fruitless efforts of the ruler of that sterile land. Welch frames the episode, in which the narrator reflects on the death of his father, First Raise, and on his unachieved dreams of an elk hunt, between the flight of three mallards and the squawking of a magpie. Like other elements in Welch's setting, these birds, whether regarded as symbolic or not, remain distant from the narrator and therefore underline his lack of connection, not only with his romantic love (Agnes) and familial love (notably, his mother), but also with his environment, or nature.

Much of the remainder of the first part of the novel concerns the narrator's resentment over his mother's sudden marriage to Lame Bull, who is eight years younger than she and who appears to be motivated by his interest in her ranch. Teresa, the narrator's mother, like Mose, his dead brother, possesses a name that connects her to the Anglo world; presumably (given her loyal Catholicism), she is named after St. Teresa of Avila. Throughout the novel, the naming of the Indian characters alternates between Native (Lame Bull, Yellow Calf) and Anglo (Teresa, Mose), which reflects the important theme of confused identity and the dilemma of being Native American in Euro-America. Teresa's attitude toward Indians is indicative of the problem. When the narrator suggests that his father stayed away from their home because of her, Teresa counters that "he was a wanderer—just like you, just like all these damned Indians" (20). But when he insists that he does not blame her, she responds with an obvious self-contradiction: "There is nothing wrong with being an Indian" (20). The narrator's distance from his tribal traditions may be implicit, too, in his suggestion that Agnes was "just a girl I picked up and brought home, a fish for dinner" (22). As Welch was to point out a dozen years later in *Fools Crow,* traditionally Blackfeet did not eat fish.

Something of Welch's understated humor is apparent in the dialogue in section 11 that follows Lame Bull's confrontation with Raymond Long Knife while mowing hay. He is speaking with Ferdinand Horn and his wife, who have visited primarily in order to inform the narrator that they saw Agnes in Malta that day. (Some readers, in fact, might detect a comical connection between Ferdinand Horn and Ferdinand, the gentle bull of the children's story and the subject of a Disney cartoon.)

"That's another thing the matter with these Indians."
He nodded gravely.
Ferdinand Horn nodded gravely.
"They get too damn tricky for their own good."
Ferdinand Horn's wife nodded gravely.
"On the other hand, where would we be without Long Knife? He's not a bad worker and he used to be a champion—saddle bronc."
The chair in the living room squeaked. (30)

The squeaking chair is the response from the narrator's otherwise incommunicative grandmother, who, he says elsewhere, "had told me many things, many stories from her early life" (34). Supposedly, the widowed grandmother had Teresa late in life by a half-white drifter named Doagie, but the mystery of her lineage, and therefore of the narrator's, is solved only near the end of the novel, when it is revealed that her father was actually old Yellow Calf. Consequently, the narrator is not mixed-blood, and the metaphorical winter that distances him from his heritage is dissolved.

In the last six sections of part 1 the narrator goes to Malta to track down his girlfriend, initiating a series of fantasy-like or surreal encounters that absorb the core of the novel and run throughout part 2. Like the narrator, the so-called Airplane Man he encounters at a bar is adrift in the world, every bit as much of a wanderer as the narrator and his father and "all these damned Indians," as Teresa proclaimed earlier. Part 2 does not begin where part 1 leaves off, however, as the narrator, having returned to the ranch, converses with blind, old Yellow Calf in his shack about three miles away. The old man tells the narrator "the world is cockeyed" (68) and advises, "sometimes it seems that one has to lean into the wind to stand straight" (69). Once again, the transition between sections is abrupt, as the reader leaves Yellow Calf in the last sentence of section 18 "facing off toward the river, listening to two magpies argue," and starts section 19, "Lame Bull jerked the pickup up the incline and pointed it west toward Harlem" (70). In short, Welch does not offer the sort of transitions one might anticipate in more conventional fiction. It is clear from what Lame Bull says, however, that the narrator is continuing his pursuit of Agnes, this time heading westward, and when he meets a woman named Malvina in a bar in Harlem, he rides with her to Havre, about fifty miles farther west, where Agnes is supposed to be.

After an unsatisfactory sexual encounter with Malvina, the narrator moves through Havre in a blur of surreal events that echo and outstrip those that make up the sections in part 1 in Malta. Once more, he encounters the Airplane Man who appears to be on the lam, and once again there is talk of fishing, despite the narrator's insistence that there are no fish to be found in the river. When he asks an old man at a café for confirmation, however, the "old-timer" laughs and drops dead, plunging "facedown into the oatmeal" (88). To this extraordinary event, the narrator merely responds by tapping him on the shoulder and ascertaining that "he was dead all right" (88). Welch sustains this absurdist comedy throughout the remainder of part 2, as the Airplane Man wins boxes of chocolates and a purple teddy bear by gambling at punch-board, and the narrator follows him through the streets toting his prizes. The Airplane Man, who seems quite paranoid, claims to be heading for the Canadian border, and he invites the narrator into his intrigue, but as the tension rises, the narrator finds himself increasingly drawn back to the memory of his brother's fatal accident twenty years earlier. That accident, which the narrator has repressed and over which he feels guilty, appears by bits and pieces throughout the novel, and it is obvious that he will not be healed of the psychological distance he feels until he comes to terms with it. He bears a physical reminder of the accident in his injured knee. Not coincidentally, the accident occurred in the winter, when the boys were herding cows near the highway, so it, too, contributes to the winter that is "in" his blood.

Near the end of part 2 the narrator finally encounters Agnes, but he fails to get her to come with him, and the intrigue involving the Airplane Man ends with his arrest by the highway patrol, but Welch offers no explanation. The narrator meanwhile finds himself being tended to by a woman named Marlene, who becomes, in effect, another version of Malvina. Although his sexual encounter with Marlene might be considered more satisfactory than that with Malvina, it does not provide the narrator with whatever it is he needs. Clearly, his pursuit of sexual gratification is a substitute for, or a diversion from, confrontation of the traumatic event that has frozen his feelings and his capacity for meaningful action: "And I was staring at the sobbing woman with the same lack of emotion, the same curiosity, as though I were watching a bug floating motionless down an irrigation ditch, not yet dead but having decided on death" (123). Part 2 ends with the narrator leaving Havre and feeling the bump on his nose that he got after being punched while trying to get Agnes to leave a bar; therefore, in effect, he is pretty much where he began at the start of the novel, when he was nursing a black eye.

The sometimes nightmarish experiences that have accumulated, however, have gradually imposed the repressed memory on the narrator's consciousness, and as he returns home in part 3, he needs only one decisive event to bring out the remainder of the tragic accident that has left him unable to get on with his life. Presumably, that event is the death of his grandmother, for even though he expresses no great remorse and in fact finds it "good to be home" (133), it is only after participating in what some readers have seen as a sort of mock communion (wine and Fritos) with Teresa and Lame Bull and then digging the grave that the remainder of the episode concerning Mose's death spills out, and he is able to "absolve" his old horse, Bird, of any burden of guilt in the affair. At the end of part 3, it remains only for the narrator himself to be absolved of "the final burden of guilt" (146), and that is the subject of part 4.

The fourth part begins with the narrator's report of his grandmother's death to old Yellow Calf, who solves the mystery of the narrator's bloodline. Yellow Calf's story involves the historical winter of the title, the so-called Starvation Winter of 1883–84. In the process of explaining how the old lady's husband, Chief Standing Bear, was killed on a raid against the Gros Ventres, Yellow Calf reveals that he is not Gros Ventre himself, but Blackfeet, like the narrator's grandmother and Standing Bear; moreover, he reveals that he, and not the half-breed Doagie, was Teresa's father. The grandmother had been left alone by the soldiers at the Gros Ventre reservation because they did not realize she was Blackfeet. (Although the Fort Belknap reservation, where this novel is set, remains the center of the Gros Ventres today, many Blackfeet and members of other tribes, notably Assiniboine, who were traditional enemies, reside there amicably). That Yellow Calf is in fact Teresa's father is something the narrator knows only "by instinct" as they laugh together, but it is "as though it was his blood in my veins that told me" (160). In effect, the narrator has experienced a sort of blood transfusion.

The short epilogue provides a kind of dark or absurd comic ending for the novel, as the narrator describes Lame Bull at the burial looking "pretty good" in "his shiny green suit" (173) and himself wearing a suit that had belonged to his father. He concludes, "Teresa wore a black coat" and "the old lady wore a shiny orange coffin" (174). After jumping up and down on the coffin in order to get it to fit into the hole, Lame Bull eulogizes the grandmother as "[n]ot the best mother in the world . . . but a good mother, notwithstanding," and as a woman "who could take it and dish it out" (175) and "who never gave anybody any crap" (176). The novel ends with the narrator throwing the old woman's tobacco pouch into the grave, a gesture that has given rise to some speculation as to whether it signifies his rejection of the past, or his honoring of the tradition of burying an important possession with the deceased.

One could combine both of the last two parts and the epilogue and still have a section that falls short of either one of the first two parts. This organization suggests either that Welch was hurrying the narrative after he finished part 2, or that he intended to speed up the pace of the novel for the reader. While the first suggestion is plausible enough, especially considering that this is a first novel, critics have so far not objected to the shortening of the last two parts, and certainly the tempo does pick up as the protagonist approaches his home, following the motif of the "homing" plot that William Bevis has found typical in the Native American novel and indicative of Indian "tribalism."[30] As the analysis above indicates, however, the "homing" plot is rather complex in this novel, involving a pattern of return and departure, and it concludes in the epilogue with the protagonist's intention to leave home once again, either to have his knee operated on or to resume his pursuit of Agnes and perhaps ask her to marry him. The pattern is as follows (numbers indicate sections): coming home (1); heading east toward Malta by way of Dodson (13); returning home to visit Yellow Calf (18); heading west to Havre in pursuit of Agnes (19); returning home to find grandmother has died (33); planning to leave home to have an operation or to resume pursuit of Agnes (epilogue).

While *Winter in the Blood* certainly is not a one-character novel, understanding it does involve coming to terms with the first-person narrator and protagonist, who is always at the focal point. Welch used as an ironic working title "The Only Good Indian" (". . .is a dead Indian," to complete the quotation ascribed to both General Philip Sheridan and to Lt. Col. George A. Custer), and in his comments that accompany his excerpt in the *South Dakota Review,* he describes his unnamed protagonist as "a do-nothing low-life, but in the end, he will discover that he is human if insignificant."[31] While the twenty or so pages from the opening sections of the novel changed considerably from their public debut, Welch has not significantly altered his attitude (or "interpretation") of the protagonist. In 1982 he told Bill Bevis, "The character was just an average guy, basically, and he drank too much—he was bored. There was an innate dissatisfaction with his life. He wanted something better but he didn't know what it was. These are really common problems."[32] Bevis, however, argued that although that may have been Welch's intention with the character and while that character may have "average problems," his "consciousness is extraordinary. I think every reader feels he's in the presence of a speaker who is very smart, very observant, and very articulate. So, in that sense, mentally, he's never an average Joe."[33] This response implicitly introduces what has become an important theoretical issue in recent literary criticism: in short, is the author an authority on his or her own text? Bevis's response to Welch's portrayal of the narrator in the novel suggests that the author is not an authority, or at least not necessarily. Welch's response to

Bevis was, "at the risk of sounding conceited, I think because I didn't know how to write a novel, I sort of wrote about me in that respect. I always saw things, you know, so I think what I did was use my consciousness through him and then put him through things that a lot of people suffer up in that area."[34] If that is in fact the case, then it is no wonder that the protagonist's thoughts often sound like those of the poet that James Welch was at the time: "I was as distant from myself as a hawk from the moon" (2); "Outside the window, a meadowlark announced the first streaks of the morning sun" (82); "and I found myself a child again, the years shed as a snake sheds its skin" (146).

But if the unnamed narrator (his surname is First Raise, but he is never mentioned by name in the novel) is, as Bevis claims, "a very sophisticated consciousness . . . so sensitive, so observant, so intelligent, so articulate, so verbal," that fact has not changed Welch's apparent view as to his circumstances at the end of the novel.[35] In an interview conducted three years after the one with Bill Bevis, Welch declared that when the protagonist stands at his grandmother's grave, in the epilogue, "I wanted to convey the sense that he was going to go on with his life, and it might not be much changed from the way it was at the beginning of the book. I believe not many of us learn from our mistakes."[36] This is, at least in part, what Welch means by saying that he wrote the novel "in a circular fashion." The interviewer persisted, "You don't see him as changing much?" Welch responded, "No. He had a few insights as a result of the things that happened to him, but the opportunities aren't great on the reservation and I think he would probably be searching still for something."[37] As to what some readers might regard as the mystery over the protagonist's name, Welch told O'Connell, "the simple truth is that for the first thirty or forty pages I didn't even think of him having a name." He then "made up a little game" for himself, whereby the narrator would have to earn his name, as in traditional tribal cultures, but "[f]or some reason I didn't feel that he was really successful in that attempt, and so I just kept him nameless."[38] A. LaVonne Ruoff, however, notes the "traditional reluctance of the Blackfeet, Gros Ventres, and Plains tribes to tell their names for fear it will bring bad luck."[39]

If one follows the implications of Welch's assessment of the narrator in *Winter in the Blood,* one must face the prospect of a protagonist in a "classic" novel being led from a sense of personal alienation and uncertain self-identity that leaves him bitter, depressed, and confused, through an epiphanic revelation that dissolves the distance he feels between himself and the world, after which the character is right back where he started. Something within us is likely to object that such an ending in "unfair," or at least that it "doesn't follow." After all he has been through, and after at last coming to terms with the long suppressed pain of his brother's death, and after the dramatic revelation of his true Blackfeet heritage, surely he must be a changed man, perhaps even radically altered. The ending we might anticipate is that he will have his knee repaired, get a good job, and marry Agnes, saving her in the process from becoming a bar-woman or a prostitute. Certainly, the narrator hints at this at the end, and as Ruoff observes, "The novel is concerned with the search for wholeness."[40] But whether he acquires that "wholeness" is debatable. Asked about his possible use of a "vision quest" in either of his first two novels, Welch, who describes himself as writing "in the

Western, European-American tradition" and not as a "traditional storyteller," denied that premise and with respect to the narrator in *Winter in the Blood,* he added, "he seems to grow a little bit as a person, but not a lot."[41] Perhaps, as Nora Baker Barry suggests, this is "a novel of survival," and merely enduring or going on with life implies successful reintegration of the main character with the world.[42] In the discussion that followed the presentation of papers at the Modern Language Association meeting in Chicago in December of 1977, Sybil Esten argued that she did not think Welch was saying "the 'Indian' situation is going to improve, culturally."[43] Paula Gunn Allen, on the other hand, saw the conclusion in a more positive light: "More important is the fact that the narrator takes an action and does something; he commits himself. . . . Also, the narrator can regenerate another generation once he understands who he is."[44] Stephen Tatum, however, finds the epilogue to be not so much ambiguous as ambivalent, and he argues that the novel's mysteries can be solved only when readers resist bourgeois "conventions of classical realism," avoid the attempt to fashion a "seamless text," and "attend to how its dissonances of form and meaning disclose the larger contradictions and ideological tensions in its social context."[45]

One explanation (of sorts) for the narrator's relatively slight, as opposed to "dramatic," change is implicit in the kind of novel Welch has told interviewers this is: "I had at the back of my mind the idea of a picaresque novel."[46] Welch was speaking in particular of the episodic and "fairly linear" nature of his plot, which does have much in common with those of novels in the picaresque tradition. Although one ought not to assume that he had a textbook knowledge, a quick survey of the most important identifying features of the subgenre suggests that *Winter in the Blood* is "picaresque" in several ways (citations are from various critical studies):

> It [the picaresque novel] is the adventurous story of a rogue's life, usually told in the first person; . . . its episodic account of wanderings, adversity, and ingenious role-playing incorporates a satiric view of society.[47]

> [*Lazarillo de Tormes* (1554)] provided the form for the future picaresque novel—an autobiographical narration with an episodic plot.[48]

> The discrete fragments into which its events are broken express anything but order. . . . Since there are no limitations of probability, the door is left open to the fantastic, the improbable, and even the weird.[49]

> Characters appear and disappear to no effect, forever forgotten. Usually the protagonist does not seek any stable relation between himself and another, as in the romance. If he does, he is usually frustrated. . . . In certain novels, however, [characters] disappear and then, mysteriously, reappear without the picaro's seeking them.[50]

The passages cited above apply so obviously to Welch's first novel that they require little elaboration. The translation of the Spanish "picaro" as "rogue" has been bandied about over the past century, with some commentators preferring "delinquent," the important point being that he is "not a vicious criminal such as a gangster or a murderer, but someone who is dishonorable and anti-social in a much less violent way."[51] The first-person narrative viewpoint is basic to the subgenre, as are such elements as apparently aimless wandering, struggling with adversity (and often losing the struggle), and confronting bizarre characters and events. The old man who dies in his bowl of oatmeal, along with women like Malvina and Marlene, exemplify the tendency for characters to appear and disappear without further comment or reflection, while the Airplane Man represents the character who disappears and then "mysteriously" reappears.

Stuart Miller indicates that "internal instability" is a significant trait of the picaro, in part because of "his inability to love, the circumstances of his origins, and his loneliness."[52] The "inner chaos"[53] of the picaresque hero often derives from confused or uncertain origins: "The unstable family situation of the picaro sends him away from home on his picaresque journey."[54] Certainly, the unnamed protagonist of Welch's novel has an uncertain genealogy, believing he is the grandson of Doagie, a half-white drifter. The issues of "origins" and of familial instability do not necessarily require that the picaro be the son (or daughter) of a prostitute, or that he be illegitimate. Clearly, the First Raise family is in disarray. But one of the most apposite characteristics of the picaresque hero, as indicated by Robert Alter, is his resistance to change, his "fixed personality": "He learns, but he does not change"; he "never substantially alters," despite his "varied experiences."[55]

Presumably, of course, Welch did not set out to devise a character who would fit some sort of picaresque paradigm, and in fact no single picaro, whether the Spanish Guzman de Alfranche or the French Gil Blas or the English Roderick Random, possesses all of the defining traits, but the narrator of *Winter in the Blood* fits well enough. Nevertheless, one must apply terms and labels judiciously. The unnamed protagonist of Welch's novel never approaches the lightheartedness or innocence often ascribed to the picaresque hero, nor does he exhibit the wit and cleverness often associated with the type. Moreover, one might argue that the satiric intent of the picaresque novel, which typically aims at such social institutions as the church or the military, is at best only implied here: the portrait of the professor from Michigan in section 32, for example, or the Catholic priest from Harlem who is Teresa's confidant, but will not allow Indians to be buried in the Catholic cemetery. Arguably, Welch's protagonist has too much depth and complexity of character to be a proper picaro; he is haunted by the past and by a vague sense of guilt that is out of keeping with the less self-conscious picaro. But above all, and despite the many comical moments in the novel, the tone never becomes truly light or playful, and the protagonist is too old to amble along with the boyish Huck Finn. Moreover, while the picaro quickly becomes adept at manipulating both people and "the system," Welch's narrator never does. Critics have in passing noted certain possibly Odyssean traits in the protagonist, but he is more suitably regarded as anti-Odyssean. While he is tempted by one Calypso or another on his journeys, Welch's narrator is more often "always at a loss" than "never at a loss," so the definitive epithet does not apply. As a literary character among characters, he is "comparable to" and "reminiscent of," but he is unique.

The critical conversations about this novel have been multifaceted, and they take their origins in observations made by book reviewers, by Welch himself, and by the critics and scholars who participated in the 1977 MLA seminar, several of whose papers were published in the spring 1978 issue of *American Indian Quarterly*. Peter G. Beidler, who organized the seminar and edited the special issue, indicates in his prefatory essay that the proposals for papers tended to fall into three principal categories: studies of imagery (distance, wind, animals); application of Blackfeet or Gros Ventre myths and traditions (the "Indianness" of the novel); and "possibilities for human development" (the narrator's search for himself, the theme of spiritual regeneration, Yellow Calf's role as teacher and healer, psychological or psychoanalytic motifs).[56] Beidler decided to select papers that dealt with two topics: "the dominant emotional condition of the narrator" (alienation) and the overall "tone" of the novel (comic, tragic, satiric, elegiac, or something else).[57] While he notes that many early reviewers saw the novel as negative in its "exploration of an American Indian wasteland," Beidler points out that participants in the seminar generally agreed the protagonist "does grow and that he has achieved a measure of wisdom by the end of the novel."[58]

Critics and readers have been divided both in their approaches to the novel and in their interpretations of it along two major axes: first, the relative importance of Blackfeet and Gros

Ventre mythology and tradition as a context from which to deal
with the novel, and second, the significance of the comic elements in the novel. Those who prefer what has been described as
"intrinsic" approaches are represented by critics like Kathleen
M. Sands, who perceives that the narrator "suffers the malaise of
modern man; he is alienated from his family, his community, his
land, and his own past."[59] That is, the dilemma is not distinctly
"Indian" in nature. (Perhaps few readers would go so far as
Reynolds Price, who asserted that it is "by no means an 'Indian
novel,'" even though his point was to emphasize that *Winter in
the Blood* is a fine novel, and not just a fine ethnic novel.) John
Scheckter, who connects his perspective with that of Peter Wild,
argues that the main characters in both *Winter in the Blood* and
The Death of Jim Loney lack awareness that they are pursuing
traditional tribal patterns and that when "the experiences of tribal
life" are "partially glimpsed by the characters," they "prove dis-
heartening to them."[60] For example, when Yellow Calf informs
the narrator of how his grandmother was rejected by her people
partly because of her beauty, the narrator objects, but all that
Yellow Calf can offer as a rationale is, "It wasn't a question of
belief, it was the way things were" (155). This example of tribal
behavior can hardly be expected to impress the alienated protagonist, and in fact, one could go so far as to argue that what Yellow Calf teaches by his own example are lessons about the value
of individual choice in opposition to tribal or communal tradition. In effect, the tribal response to the crisis of the Starvation
Winter of 1883–84 is depicted as wrong. To the extent that the
grandmother and old Yellow Calf are "survivors," as various
readers have remarked, they represent what can be achieved by

individuals in opposition to tribal tradition, as opposed to conformity, which is what all tribes demand as the "price" of community. Although Elizabeth Cook-Lynn does not refer to Welch in her essay on "the new Indian story," the implications of this approach are in keeping with her concern about "mixed-blood literature" being "characterized by excesses of individualism."[61]

At the other extreme are critics like Paul Eisenstein, who suggests that Welch may have learned from Hemingway's technique of omission (usually of an important detail in a story, which is implied but not stated): "The need to recover omitted history (and to enact the process whereby it is recovered) . . . is the governing force of the narrator's progression through, and our reading of, *Winter in the Blood*."[62] Behind the lost Indian history is "the ruling culture's politics of concealment," Eisenstein argues; therefore, implicitly, the contexts of Blackfeet and Gros Ventre mythology are essential for a full appreciation of the novel.[63] John Purdy, for example, argues that "Welch's are people who move away from a debilitating concern for self, and exemplify qualities of tribal endurance."[64] Writers like William W. Thackery and A. LaVonne Ruoff have followed this sort of "extrinsic" critical approach, which requires investigations into cultural contexts. For example, in "'Crying for Pity' in *Winter in the Blood*" Thackery describes a mystical structure for the novel that is associated with Gros Ventre age-graded societies, initiation rituals, and a vision quest; and in "Animal Allies and Transformers of *Winter in the Blood*" he delves into both Blackfeet and Gros Ventre mythology, reflecting on such matters as the taboo against eating wildfowl and its relevance to the episode in which Teresa kills Amos the duck for Thanksgiving dinner.[65]

Ruoff, in "Alienation and the Female Principle in *Winter in the Blood*," comments on the grandmother's story with respect to the traditional Blackfeet and Gros Ventre taboo against intermarriage within the band, notes Teresa's usurpation of traditionally male roles, and points to the importance of chastity among both Blackfeet and Gros Ventres when she comments on Agnes and Malvina.[66] Paula Gunn Allen has gone so far as to suggest that the alienation theme itself is "an articulation of a basic experience, one that is characteristic of the life and consciousness of the half or mixed breed."[67] She conjectures that the "preoccupation" with this theme, "in its classic dimensions of isolation, powerlessness, meaninglessness, normlessness, lowered self-esteem, and self-estrangement, accompanied by a pervasive anxiety, a kind of hopelessness, and a sense of victimization" may owe to the fact that the writers, like Welch, "are predominately breeds themselves." Such approaches to this novel, or to other Native American writing, respond implicitly to one important "requirement" of the three that Arnold Krupat has stated as essential to "the development of any critical approaches to native American literature": "there must be a knowledge of the culture whose concerns that literature expresses and addresses."[68]

Although it would be an oversimplification to categorize interpretations of the narrator's growth or progress by connecting the critic with emphasis on culturally based approaches, on the one hand, or more traditionally "literary" (or "formalistic") approaches, on the other, a brief comparison of Paula Gunn Allen's conclusions with those of Alan Velie are illustrative of the gulf that separates the camps: "In the end, it is his recognition of this [that he is "adrift in a life that lacks shape, goal, understanding, or significance"] that leads him through his impasse and allows him to reintegrate his personality around realistic perceptions of himself and the reality he inhabits" (Allen);[69] "There is no resolution at the end of the novel, and unlike Abel [the main character in Momaday's *House Made of Dawn*], the narrator does not find himself, or develop a new sense of identity" (Velie).[70] Although Allen attends to the cultural circumstances of Welch's novels, she finds that "his novels reach resolution in singularly 'white' ways."[71] And although he attempts to use cultural contexts (specifically, in this case, the trickster myth) to combat a worst-possible-case scenario whereby Indian characters are sometimes criticized for being alienated, passive, violent loners and losers,[72] Velie does not conclude that the narrator experiences the sort of self-discovery that would lead him to a new identity or that would put him in the position, as Allen describes it, "to make plans for a future that will not be as blighted as his past."[73]

That there are in fact comic elements in *Winter in the Blood* has been acknowledged from the outset, but whether it is genuinely humorous or funny, on the one hand, or in fact bitterly ironic and darkly comic, on the other, remains an important topic for debate. As Welch himself noted, "I intentionally put comic stuff in there just to alleviate that vision of alienation and purposelessness, aimlessness,"[74] but that statement does not necessarily amount to a declaration that the novel is a comedy. If one follows the view that comedies begin in disintegration (the "distance," for example, that the narrator mentions five times in a space of ten lines on the second page) and ends in reintegration (the implied dissolving of that feeling in the epilogue), then the novel could be described as a comedy. But if one ascribes to Byron's view that all comedies end in either a wedding or a banquet (that is, in a celebratory and communal ritual), then the novel is a comedy only from a perverse or ironic perspective, inasmuch as the last scene, even though it brings the cast of characters together as comedy traditionally does, is a funeral. Andrew Horton asserts that the humor is "bitter and ironic rather than funny in a pure comic sense";[75] that even though the narrator shares some characteristics of the trickster and joker, "there are few laughs" in the book;[76] and that although the funeral is "farcical" in some ways, "real laughter is not possible" and "no clear catharsis has taken place."[77] From Horton's use of the term "catharsis" one may infer that he detects tragic elements in the novel, and Nora Baker Barry goes so far as to argue that the bitter and ironic humor does not alter the tone, which she finds to be "elegiac."[78]

At the opposite pole are critics such as Alan R. Velie, who describes *Winter in the Blood* as "a masterpiece of comic fiction" and observes that "Welch's humor varies from raucous farce to subtle satire, and it informs every corner of the novel."[79] Despite his efforts to oppose the limited, "partial vision" caused by "the way Anglos read about Indians" in his essay on the trickster figure in novels by Momaday and Welch,[80] Velie has been particularly associated with the effort to "anglicize" Welch.[81] Kenneth Lincoln focuses on the scatological humor in the novel and describes it as a "contrary humor" that "can be mistaken for bitterness."[82] For Lincoln, the novel offers "a real cartoon of American manhood, beneath which runs a critical set of lessons,"[83] and it is "a bold comic experiment in realistic fiction" that involves "desacralized humor."[84] Lincoln does not go so far as Charles R. Larson, however, who praises the "relaxed" style and tone of the novel and compliments "the general feeling of goodwill that Welch displays toward his characters and their lives."[85] "Laughter in this novel," according to Lincoln, "can be taken as an absurdist cry of survival."[86] Not surprisingly, at least one critic has seen the novel as "a tragicomedy."[87] Peter Wild, who has also been accused of opposing "Indianist" readings of Welch's novels,[88] suggests, "what counts is that the narrator realizes that he has been taking his harsh world too seriously," and "this realization leads to a release of tension in his life, a small and unprofound but important victory for the troubled individual as he grows from an uneasy childishness toward a more relaxed maturity."[89]

Whether in fact *Winter in the Blood* will survive its moment and become not just a (or "the") "Classic Tale of Indian Life Today" is impossible to say with absolute confidence, but the prospects are very good. Attempting to cover both extremes of the critical controversy over the novel, Professors Jim Charles and Richard Predmore have published observations on their team-teaching approach to *Winter in the Blood* by way of integrating two "diverse literary critical theories," the "sociocultural" and the "formalistic."[90] In presenting the novel to their upper-level English majors, Charles adopted the former avenue, emphasizing such matters as the role of the trickster character, the motif of intertribal conflict, and the importance of oral traditions, while Predmore focused on such traditional, New Critical elements as imagery and symbolism. Critics like Louis Owens, with his references to T. S. Eliot's *The Waste Land,* Saul Bellow's *Henderson the Rain King,* and Terry Eagleton's "Brecht and Rhetoric," are reading the novel from one perspective,[91] while critics like A. LaVonne Ruoff, William Thackery, and Jack L. Davis, who sees the protagonist as having "retribalized himself against all odds" and as "proof that assimilation is not inevitable,"[92] are reading it from another, but perhaps ultimately compatible, viewpoint.

CHAPTER FOUR

The Tragedy of Jim Loney

James Welch's second novel, *The Death of Jim Loney,* was published in 1979 to less than ecstatic reviews, and it has not generated the amount or quality of critical response that has greeted *Winter in the Blood. The Death of Jim Loney,* although it differs drastically in tone, is in many ways a close partner with Welch's first novel, similar in both length and construction, and in its intent focus on a single character who is ill at ease in the world. A quick survey of the critical response to *The Death of Jim Loney* indicates a gradual but steady increase in its appeal, and William Bevis has suggested recently that "because of the crucible it plunges us into," it is "increasingly admired by those who teach Native American literature."[1]

Anatole Broyard began his scathing review in the *New York Times,* "James Welch may have the makings of a good novelist, but it's hard to tell, because he has shrouded himself in cliches of a certain kind of contemporary writing."[2] Broyard described Loney as another "hero of hopelessness, . . . as static as the old wooden Indian in front of the cigar store." Even more sympathetic commentators have labeled the novel "unrelievedly grim" and "unrelievedly bleak."[3] On the other hand, C. M. Klein found that the novel "fulfills the earlier promise of *Winter in the Blood*" and even felt that Jim Loney was "a more sympathetic character" than the earlier protagonist, "more of an everyman."[4] Kathleen Sands called it an "unsettling yet strangely, satisfying novel," and in its use of "dark" irony, "ultimately consoling."[5] Peter Wild, however, devotes about twice as much text to *Winter in the Blood* in his pamphlet on James Welch, and he treats *The Death of Jim Loney* as melodrama emanating from "the ghoulish world of television soap opera."[6] Wild disputes "admirers" of native American fiction who "strain to justify what they see as the literary virtues" of the novel, repudiates those who resort to ethnography to find evidence of "Indianness" in it, and concludes that "ultimately it is a badly flawed novel, not worthy of his best work."[7]

Although this novel has not drawn the acclaim of *Winter in the Blood,* Kathryn Vangen's statement that it "has attracted none of the attention of its predecessor" is demonstrably erroneous.[8] For writers, as for other artists, it may be better to be chided, or even panned, than to be ignored. Moreover, Welch's supporters have continued to outnumber his detractors considerably. Frederick Turner, writing in the *Nation,* praised Welch for resisting the impulse "to capitalize in a personal way on this ethnic heritage, rightly wishing to be thought of as a writer, period," and he insisted that *The Death of Jim Loney* should not be categorized as "Indian writing": Welch "is writing about life in America, about our shared moral landscape" in language that is "shaved to the bone."[9] Paul N. Pavich praised the style as "lean" and "concise," and he concluded that the novel made "an unforgettable statement about the destruction of the human spirit."[10] Nevertheless, there has remained around this novel an aura of uncertainty, as if even those critics and scholars who are delving deeply into it have misgivings. William Bevis, for example, confesses that he found it "at first a most uncomfortable book,"[11] and Kathleen Sands is at some pains both to prove that it is "definitely" an Indian novel and that while it is "undeniably a novel of alienation," it is "not a novel of emptiness or despair."[12]

Clearly Jim Loney, whose name, as various readers have observed, suggests both "lone" and "loony," and includes the author's first name,[13] is something of a problem character, and Wild goes so far as to insist that he "evokes pity rather than sympathy" and is "a pathetic, rather than a tragic figure."[14] In many ways *The Death of Jim Loney* complements *Winter in the Blood;* that is, they form a sort of antithetical pair. The protagonist of Welch's first novel, for example, discovers that he is not related, through his grandmother, to a half-white drifter, but that he is (apparently) a full-blood Blackfeet. Jim Loney, however, is of mixed blood, and he moves uneasily between the Indian and the Anglo worlds. While the unnamed protagonist of *Winter in the Blood* has a mother (with whom he does not get along very well) and a deceased father, Loney has a father (with whom he scarcely communicates) and no mother (whether she is still alive is uncertain). While the protagonist in *Winter in the Blood* appears to be inept in his dealings with women, Loney apparently is loved by his girlfriend Rhea and is admired by his sister Kate, and Kate herself constitutes one aspect of the antithetical structure, inasmuch as she is at least available as a supportive sibling for her brother, whereas the narrator of *Winter in the Blood* is haunted by the death of his brother Mose. Both novels are set on the Montana Highline, but the narrator of *Winter in the Blood* is almost always in motion, although his tether is fairly short, reaching only from Havre to the west and Malta to the east (a span of about ninety miles). The reader is told that "[s]ometimes on Saturday they [Loney and Rhea] drove to Havre for a matinee" (13) and like the narrator of *Winter in the Blood,* he spent some time in Seattle, but Jim Loney's world is narrowly constricted to Harlem and the Gros Ventre reservation at Fort Belknap. Finally, while *Winter in the Blood* moves toward a resolution appropriate to comedy, in which the protagonist returns to the community or family, *The Death of Jim Loney* ends with the protagonist's violent and indeed tragic death.

The great world outside the reservation constantly calls to both protagonists, sometimes very obviously, as when Rhea urges Loney to accompany her to a new life in Seattle, while his sister tries to convince him to come with her to Washington, D.C.; sometimes more subtly, by implicit distance, as when the narrator in *Winter in the Blood* finds himself in front of the Coast-to-Coast store in Havre. In fact, although the place names along the Highline could be argued to figure only coincidentally in these novels, most readers will find themselves at one time or another reflecting on the distant, exotic places they augur: Harlem (the Black and Spanish ghettoes of New York City, and more distantly, the city in Holland where the name originated), Havre (the French port on the English Channel), and Malta (the small island in the Mediterranean associated with a crusading order and with a spirited defense against Nazi air attack during World War II). It is as if the settlers themselves felt called upon to hearken, perhaps with conscious irony, to a world of great places beyond the small towns of northern Montana (about seventy miles east of Malta lies the town of Glasgow, population about 4,500). Part of the general "malaise" (7, 25) and restlessness (20) that affects both Rhea and Loney, and presumably the narrator of *Winter in the Blood* as well, owes to the limited potential such small towns offer. The troubled Jim Loney mumbles in his sleep, "I'm small" (32), and a few pages later he reflects that he has "become something of a nonperson, as one only can in a small town, a small town in Montana" (41). Some readers have been annoyed about Loney's apparent anomie and lack of will, his tendency to feel sorry for himself, and his futile drinking, but as this passage demonstrates, the protagonist is sensitive and perceptive as to the nature of his dilemma.

In one of the most ambitious critical essays devoted to *The Death of Jim Loney* Robert M. Nelson sets out to demonstrate that "landscape" functions in the novel as "the source of cure for psychological and spiritual alienation."[15] Under the circumstances, perhaps it is more than coincidence that the Harlem of Welch's novel, which lies just north of the Gros Ventre reservation, is itself a sort of ghetto. Rhea, Loney's Anglo girlfriend from Texas, can escape that ghetto for Seattle, and Kate, Loney's thoroughly assimilated sister, has used her education to escape to Washington, D.C. But Loney's quest for a "vision of generative spirit"[16] will lead him, appropriately, to Mission Canyon, which is located at the southern extreme of the Fort Belknap reservation in the Little Rockies, yet another ironically, diminished reference to place in the novel.

The Death of Jim Loney is also constructed similarly to *Winter in the Blood;* that is, it is built of lengthy parts subdivided into short chapters (or more aptly, "sections") that rarely run more than five pages. But while *Winter in the Blood* is divided into four rather unbalanced parts (forty-two consecutively numbered sections) and an epilogue, *The Death of Jim Loney* is more tautly designed: three parts of approximately sixty pages each, with the sections, ranging from twenty-one in part 3 to twenty-four in part 2, renumbered in each part. The overall effect of the architectonic design is a sort of symmetry that suggests Welch's developing control over plot structure. The climactic event in the novel, Loney's apparently accidental killing of his friend Myron Pretty Weasel while they are hunting, occurs at the end of the second part. As in *Winter in the Blood,* transitions between sections are often abrupt, signaling shifts in the consciousness of the main character and sometimes, in *The Death of Jim Loney,* shifts in consciousness from one character to another

Appropriately, the reader first encounters Loney by himself at a local Harlem football game in which the home team is narrowly defeated. Perhaps the breath from the athletes in the rainy, late October air triggers Loney's memory of a biblical passage that haunts him: "Turn away from man in whose nostrils is breath, for of what account is he?" This verse from Isaiah 2:22 haunts Loney, who wonders whether the warning against trusting in man instead of the Lord is directed at "the players, the people around him, or himself."[17] He decides that the passage is "wrong" or that he has gotten it wrong and there is "no sense to it." Later in the novel, however, he cites the same passage to his white girlfriend Rhea and confesses that he has not looked it up because he is "afraid" he will find it, "and it will be bad" (105). Significantly, although Rhea identifies the source of the passage in Isaiah, she neither explains its implications nor tries to allay his fear. Had Loney looked up the verse, he would have discovered that it appears in a chapter concerning an apocalyptic vision of "the last days," in which "the Lord's house shall be established in the mountains, and shall be exalted above the hills; and all nations shall flow into it" (2:2). On that day, when "all shall beat their swords into plowshares, and their spears into pruning hooks" (2:4), the house of Jacob, which has bowed before Philistine idols, will be humbled. In other words, there is implicit consolation in that chapter of Isaiah, particularly for people like Loney who have not been numbered among the lofty and haughty. As will be demonstrated hereafter, chapter 2 of Isaiah also contains passages that foreshadow Loney's eventual fate. The worshiping of false gods is presumably what causes the white-dominated world around Jim Loney to be "fallen," a spiritually barren wasteland that prompts such representatives of white colonialism as Rhea and the police officer Painter Barthelme to want to be elsewhere.

The passage that Loney recalls from his Catholic boarding-school days vies with a visionary bird, large and dark, that readers generally associate with his latent native self. Loney sees the bird for the first time in the novel as he lights a cigarette and his hands shake: "Like the trembling, the bird was not new. It came every night now. It was a large bird and dark. It was neither graceful nor clumsy, and yet it was both" (20). The bird sometimes soars powerfully, and other times seems ready to fall from the air in its awkwardness. The inconsistency of the bird's flight obviously reflects Loney's unstable condition in the world, and as some readers have suggested, it might well be the sort of spirit animal Loney needs and would have acquired had he been fortunate enough to have experienced a traditional vision quest. Under the circumstances, however, the visionary bird confuses him as much as the lines of scripture.

Loney is also thrown into a state of frustrating ambivalence because of the four women in his life, two from the past and two from the present. From his past, the woman "he had tried hardest to love" (51) is an "aunt" with whom he lived for a couple of years when he was about twelve, after his white father and Indian mother deserted him and his sister. He associates the woman, whose name he is sure began with S and who turns out to have been his father's lover, with the Catholic church, butterscotch pudding, and cocoa; and when he recalls trying to comfort her one Christmas Eve, he reflects that "he had felt like a man" (51). Clearly, then, it is not so much the loss of his father that has deprived Loney of his manhood, as the loss of his full-blood Gros Ventre mother, Eletra Calf Looking; and although he eventually attempts to talk with his father, Ike, all he wants is information about his mother. In effect, the motif implicit in the novel is not the conventional European search-for-father, but a search-for-mother. Everywhere Loney goes, he appears to be reaching out to women for consolation and for the mothering of which he has been deprived. In one of his many troubling dreams, Loney encounters a beautiful young Indian mother dressed in traditional regalia at a cemetery weeping over the loss of her son. When he asks her identity, she tells him she is "[a] mother who is no longer a mother" (34). This visionary likeness of his own mother is not the only mother figure Loney encounters, however, because he is inclined to think of nearly all women in maternal terms. For example, as he reflects on the "hardness" of "bar women," he finds himself wondering "what they were like at home, if they sent kids off to school in the morning, if they made cakes" (36). Later, he is drawn to a woman who has "no apparent husband" but "two small boys" (46). She is out hanging clothes, and Loney feels "calmed and cheered" by her presence without knowing why.

Perhaps predictably, the two women who are a present part of Loney's life, his beautiful sister Kate, a successful career woman who lives in Washington, D.C., and his lover Rhea Davis, a local schoolteacher and former socialite from Dallas with an M.A. in English from Southern Methodist University, both tend to mother him in various ways. Welch alters his narrative viewpoint from third-person limited in *Winter in the Blood,* which means that the reader is privy only to the narrator's thoughts and feelings, to third-person omniscient in *The Death of Jim Loney,* which means that the reader is occasionally aware of what other characters are thinking or how they feel about what is going on around them. Consequently, characters other than the protagonist are presented more thoroughly, and readers acquire an awareness of them that might be described as more "intimate" than that which they have of such characters as Teresa, Lame Bull, and Malvina in *Winter in the Blood.* For example, the first three sections of *The Death of Jim Loney* focus strictly on Loney's perceptions and feelings, but the fourth section shifts to Rhea awakening and feeling a sense of "malaise" about her life after two years in Harlem (7). Once Loney arrives, in the next section, Welch informs readers of the thoughts and emotional responses of both characters, but Rhea dominates several sections of all three parts and emerges as a more fully realized character than Kate, who appears only briefly in the second part of the novel.

In the fourth section of part 1, in what amounts to a sort of interior monologue, Rhea, who is twenty-nine, envisions herself as a woman of "passion" with "big white teeth" that could "bite through a tree," and she caps off this observation with a growl (8). When Loney appears, she tells him, "Sometimes I think I would just like to take a bite of you" (12). Her aggressive nature hardly equips her to play the role of the nurturing woman Loney appears to desire, and she clearly dominates the relationship. Moreover, Rhea is distinctly out of place in the small, isolated town of Harlem, having envisioned Montana with images drawn from Glacier Park, but having found herself "in country that was all sky and flat land . . . Big Sky . . . with a vengeance" (11). Her severely limited understanding of Loney's dilemma is illustrated by Rhea's facile observation that he is "so lucky to have two sets of ancestors. Just think, you can be Indian one day and white the next. Whichever suits you" (14). Loney's reaction, which he does not voice to her, is that it would be preferable to have just one set of ancestors and that either one "would be nicer than being a half-breed" (14). This is not to say, however, that Rhea is insensitive to Loney's predicament, as she has written to his sister about his drinking and "his desire to isolate himself," which she describes accurately as "a crisis of spirit" (25).

Kate's letter to Rhea, which is described as "crisp, businesslike" (25), expresses her plan to take her brother back to Washington, D.C., with her, and Rhea recognizes this as a challenge to her own scheme, which is to get him to accompany her to the "lush greenery" of Seattle (26). Neither of the women appears to be much concerned with Jim Loney's preferences, and while he sleeps, Rhea reflects, "She was used to men doing foolish things for her; sometimes she made them do foolish things" (31). Rhea's superficiality is perhaps best revealed in solipsistic self-presentation: "She wondered how she looked, drink in one hand, cigarette in the other. . . . She was at home. And not at home. But at least, she thought, I am something wherever I am" (32). As opposed, that is, to Jim Loney, who comes to a party at Rhea's house wanting to tell her that "no one knew him anymore" (41). When she proposes relocating to Seattle, which Loney recalls vaguely from his basic training at Fort Lewis sixteen year earlier, he remembers that the city "scared him" (44).

As the first part of the novel ends, it is Thanksgiving Day, and Loney discovers his dog Swipesy dead and frozen into the mud. Seven-year-old Amos After Buffalo watches Loney pry the dog loose and then advises him to bury it somewhere to the south in the Little Rockies, which is sacred land for the Gros Ventres. This is one of several foreshadowing events that echo throughout the novel, for it is in the Little Rockies that Jim Loney will eventually die. As Loney drives toward Havre to meet his sister's airplane, he hopes for "some sort of controlled oblivion, if such a state existed" (59).

Part 2 opens with a scene featuring the police officer Painter Barthelme, a transplanted Californian who, like Rhea, feels out of place on the Montana Highline. The scene then abruptly shifts to Kate's arrival at the airport, complete with "authentic" squash blossom necklace, which she bought from the woman who made it "right from the heart of Navaho country" (63). In effect, the thoroughly assimilated Kate Loney is as much a tourist in Indian country as any white person would be. Immediately, she begins to take over and attempt to organize her brother's life: "She was here and she knew what to do. She sat him down and put her leather briefcase on his lap. Then she walked over to the car rental counter. She didn't bother to ask him if he had brought his" (64). Of course Loney *has* brought his car, an old '64 Chevrolet, but perhaps the most significant gesture in this passage is Kate's placing of her briefcase on her brother's lap, a subtle and probably unconscious act that asserts her power and her success in the outside world. When she meets with Rhea the next day, both women realize that they are "in competition" for Jim Loney (68).

In the second part the reader is also introduced to Ike Loney, Jim and Kate's alcoholic white father, who broods over his wife who left him some forty years ago, and to Myron Pretty Weasel, a prosperous high school friend and former basketball teammate of Jim Loney. Pretty Weasel's mother, a grade school principal in Billings, has also left the family, but while Loney's mother left him when he was about four years old, Pretty Weasel's did not leave until he was in his junior year of high school, and he has emerged from the experience without being traumatized. In a curious passage that has not drawn critical attention, Welch implies that Pretty Weasel's friendship with Jim Loney, who he admired as "the smart one" in high school, was more than the ordinary sort that typifies high school buddies: "Once in a game Pretty Weasel had broken toward the free-throw line and Loney had looked right at him before passing and Pretty Weasel fell in love right on the spot" (82). The provocative implications of this assertion are quickly averted when Pretty Weasel gets hit in the face with the ball and gets a bloody nose, but his obvious affection for Jim

Loney makes his playful "grab for Loney's nuts" (114) late in part 2 more suggestive than it might otherwise have been.

By the middle of part 2, Kate has given up on her effort to take her brother back to Washington with her, leaving him to Rhea's care. Curiously, Kate refers to Jim as "something of a toy," but Rhea, perceiving that they both love him, insists, "Please don't think he's a toy to me" (85), although she admits that at first he seemed just a "diversion" to her (86). That either of the two women who profess to love him would ever have regarded him as a toy suggests their inability to be of much use to him in his ordeal. Kate is able to identify Sandra for Jim before she leaves, but she is not able to provide her brother with much solace, despite the joy he feels when he tells her he loves her. What Jim Loney admires most in his sister is her "ability to live in the present" (88), but faced with an unattainable past and an uncertain future, the present is all that he has. Ironically, as Loney is well aware, he cannot live comfortably in the present, and he cannot accept Rhea's invitation to "escape" (87) with her to Seattle. Although Rhea does appear in the third part of the novel, she pronounces their relationship "finished" (106) before Loney goes on the fateful hunting trip with Pretty Weasel. Significantly, their parting has much to do with place, as Rhea tells Jim: "This is your country, isn't it? It means a great deal to you" (106). Loney agrees that it is his country, even though he does not understand it and believes he will die in it. Rhea can only regard this attitude as "limiting" (107), and later in the novel she relishes the thought of being "on the road" (134).

When Pretty Weasel tells Loney that he returned to Harlem after playing basketball at the University of Wyoming because he got tired of all that "Indian bullshit" (101), Loney remembers that when he was in the army people called him "Chief" even though "he was only half Indian," and he reflects that "He never felt Indian" (102). He then recalls the family of Emil Cross Guns, who followed the traditional ways, but with the old man's death, "everything was changed and the old ones did not exist" (102). Clearly, then, although Loney feels himself to be neither white nor Indian, he feels strong ties to his native heritage, arguably much stronger ties to the remnants of tribal culture than to the white world, which is represented by such conventional values as mobility and the premise that moving from one place to another will almost certainly improve one's life.

The night before the hunt Loney lies in bed dreading the dawn and thinking, "After tomorrow I will have no future. . . . After tomorrow's slim purpose I will simply exist" (108). He then lapses into a dream, or perhaps a vision, in which his father appears with his sixteen-gauge shotgun and hands it to him, then disappears. Loney pursues his phantom father into the freshly fallen snow, only to encounter a phantom of his dead dog Swipesy, which also vanishes. The next day as he and Pretty Weasel drive toward the hunting area, Loney gazes at the motionless river and tells himself that it looks "aimless and malevolent" (113), like his own life. Only as his life approaches its tragic end does Loney find himself in harmony with the landscape.

Pretty Weasel sights the "dark animal" at about two hundred yards, and it behaves strangely for a deer, moving its head up and down rapidly and dropping "to all fours" (117); that is, it behaves very much like a bear. When Loney asks if that is what it was, Pretty Wesel says yes, even though there are not supposed to be bears in the area. As he waits for his friend to move in on the animal, Loney cannot help thinking of George Yellow Eyes, a former basketball teammate they had talked about, and he wonders why he has kept the news of his death to himself. Even more significant is the fact that he never told his sister that their mother took up with Yellow Eyes' father after she left them. After she left Yellow Eyes' father, Loney reflects, "she became a dream that one wishes to forget," yet "not a dream at all," but "the stuff of which dreams are made. A real dream made of shit" (119). The painful memory is disrupted by gunfire as Pretty Weasel shoots at the animal, which Loney still assumes is a bear. His vision obscured by the cattails and the blinding sun flashing off the freshly fallen snow, Loney moves toward the place where the animal entered, and he whistles a couple of times, but he forgets the complete code he and Pretty Weasel used when they were kids hunting pheasant: "Then he heard the brittle crashing of the dry stalks and he saw the darkness of it, its immense darkness in that dazzling day, and he thrust the gun to his cheek and he felt the recoil and he saw the astonished look on Pretty Weasel's face as he stumbled two steps back and sat down in the crackling cattails" (120).

When Loney looks at the bear tracks, he finds they are filled with snow, and at this point the shooting still appears to be accidental. Nevertheless, he throws away the rifle Pretty Weasel loaned him and runs, thinking of heading for Canada, toward a town they almost played in basketball when he was in high school, but he decides there "are no Indians there, or even half-breeds" (121), and he becomes frightened and heads back toward Harlem as part 2 ends. This appears to be the first time that

Loney directly prefers his Indian self to his white self. In effect, Jim Loney already sees himself as a "marked" man, which is not surprising, considering the distance he perceives between himself and everyone else in his world. When he reappears in the third part of the novel, two days have passed, and he assumes not only that the authorities will "call it murder," but also that the bear was not a bear, "but an agent of evil" to which he has succumbed. Welch concludes, "That it was an accident did not occur to Loney" and "That the bear . . . was simply a bear did not occur to him either" (129). In what for most rational people would be something of a quantum leap in logic, Loney accepts the notion that the shooting was somehow intentional, and he behaves accordingly. This climactic event in the novel brings about something of a dilemma for most readers: Why should Loney accept (if not welcome) guilt for what appears to be an ordinary hunting accident? After all, what motive is offered for this supposed crime?

Andrew Wiget suggests, implicitly, that Loney's motive is envy, that he sees "the emptiness of his own life heightened by the substantiality" of Pretty Weasel's.[18] Robert Franklin Gish argues that "the directing and staging of Pretty Weasel's death" is an element of Loney's "willful dramatization" and "compounding death wish."[19] William W. Bevis acknowledges that the "white existential plot" might prompt Loney to accept "responsibility for accidental murder," but he credits the poet Linda Weasel Head with suggesting to him that when Loney shoots his old friend, what he sees is "a release from the realities he cannot comprehend."[20] Louis Owens asserts, "In shooting Pretty Weasel, Loney symbolically kills the Indian potential in himself—that which could believe in the bear."[21] Only after his father fails to provide the knowledge or understanding that would be of some use from what one might call his "white potential" does Loney "take control of his destiny," according to Owens, by orchestrating his own death "by adopting a warrior's stance, by selecting and controlling the time, place, and manner of his death."[22] The critic who comes closest to embracing the Native American mythic interpretation of the event is Patricia Riley In-the-Woods, who connects the death of Myron Pretty Weasel with the ritual death of Otter in the Blackfeet "earth-diver" myth of the recreation of the earth after the flood. She suggests that Pretty Weasel "re-creates a bear" and Loney believes he sees a bear and shoots it: "But the bear has shifted its shape, and it is Pretty Weasel who receives the shot and is killed."[23]

Although Loney reaches out to his sister early in the third part of the novel, she is not in when he calls, and when he visits Rhea for a last night of lovemaking, he leaves confident that she has loved him, but unwilling to tell her what has happened. A later section devoted to Kate illustrates once again how distant she is from her brother, as Welch locates her in her Georgetown apartment amid her Danish furniture and "three framed paintings by an Indian artist she had met in South Dakota" (164). It may be significant that she thinks of the artist as "Indian" and not Cheyenne, for example, or Sioux. In the longest section of the novel (nine pages) Loney interrogates his father about his mother and about Sandra, but he receives no trustworthy answers, as he challenges Ike's statement that his mother is a nurse on a reservation hospital in New Mexico. Ike assumes Loney knows more than he does: "He knows his mother is crazy. He thinks I put her

in that damn bughouse" (144). Loney then confesses to his father
that he shot Pretty Weasel, at first agreeing that it might have
been accidental, but then asserting, "I think I killed him on purpose" (148). Ike's advice is for him to run, as he has done at various times himself, but Loney announces that he intends to go to
Mission Canyon in the Little Rockies, which is "part of a dim
plan that he didn't understand" (149). Fulfilling one of Loney's
dreams early in the novel, Ike offers him his shotgun, presumably to shoot grouse while he is on the run, but after he leaves the
trailer, Loney shoots out the window, injuring his father with
glass splinters and assuring himself that his father will inform the
police. Ike, in fact, not only tells the police about his injury, but
tells them about the killing of Pretty Weasel as well, and suggests
that it was not accidental.

By the time Loney enters the canyon, it is nearly Christmas,
but Welch does not make much of the date, except to observe
that Thanksgiving was "almost a month ago" (166). In all, events
in the novel cover about two months. Loney thinks about "the
Indians who had used the canyon, the hunting parties, the warriors, the women who had picked chokecherries farther up"
(168). Significantly, these thoughts make him feel "comfortable"
and unafraid. As he continues his journey, which might be described as a vision quest, in an odd way, inasmuch as the
enlightenment he seeks will make him a whole man, but will
assist him to live only for a matter of minutes, Loney thinks
more and more in a traditional way. For example, he thinks of
himself as avoiding "the whole U.S. Army" (174), and he refers to what Nora Barry has recognized as the "Lost Children"
motif in Blackfeet and Gros Ventre folklore, observing that his

acceptance of death "represents a significant moment in Loney's ascent toward his Indian identity."[24] Now Loney sees that the woman in his dream about the young mother who had lost her son "was not crazy" (perhaps an intuition as to his own mother's fate): "He did recognize her and he knew who the lost son was" (175). Loney questions his need for cigarettes, and when he drinks some Scotch, another commodity related to the white world, he finds that "it didn't taste like anything" (176). He knows there must be a place "where people bought each other drinks and talked quietly about their pasts, their mistakes and their small triumphs," but he also knows "it was not on this earth" (175).

So precise is Jim Loney's plan that he appears even to have made certain that his old basketball teammate, Quentin Doore, an Indian he regards as a bully and a "thug" (176), will take the fatal shot. That way, any potential guilt will apply to a character who might be said to deserve it. (Welch describes Doore as having "a kind of cruelty around the eyes, that set him apart from everybody, Indian and white" [161].) Loney's last thought is "this is what you wanted," and the last thing he sees is "the beating wings of a dark bird as it climbed to a distant place" (179). As Robert M. Nelson has observed, Loney's death occurs in Mission Canyon, a place sacred to the Gros Ventres, which leads him "spiritually toward complete reintegration of his life with the regenerative spirit of the land."[25] Of course the name of the canyon also reflects the Christian mission school past which he walks on his fatal journey, so that land might be regarded properly as having spiritual significance for both his Indian and his white self. Loney's death on a rocky outcropping also looks back to the haunting passage from the second chapter of Isaiah, in which the prophet advises the Hebrew people, in the verse just before the one cited in the novel (2:22), to "go into the clefts of the rocks, and into the tops of the ragged rocks, for fear of the Lord."

Most critics have concluded, as Paula Gunn Allen phrases it, that "Loney dies like a warrior, out of choice, not out of defeat. Though he could not plan or control his life, he could, finally, determine his death."[26] Allen's observations square with those of Welch, who has proposed that one constructive or positive aspect of the novel is the protagonist's "attempt to understand something of his past," and the other concerns his death: "He does orchestrate his own death. . . . He knows how his death will occur. And to me, that is a creative act and I think all creative acts are basically positive."[27] In another interview, Welch points out that "the novel is about looking back and looking forward, trying to make some sense of it all," but Loney cannot "make any discoveries about his past," and there is no epiphany as there is in *Winter in the Blood.*[28] What Jim Loney does discover about himself is that Rhea's love is insufficient (she does not, after all, appear to possess great depth of character), his sister's way of rationalizing the past and going on from there will not work for him, and life as it is (the status quo on the reservation) is meaningless. His killing of Myron Pretty Weasel, whether accidental or not, effectively closes the door on the possibility of living in and for the present, except as that might constitute life in the state prison at Deer Lodge. In effect, his response is similar to that of Othello, who also kills the only person who loves him and accepts the burden of responsibility for his act. As Welch has phrased it, the reason Loney "does what he does after killing this guy is to carry his life through to its completion.[29]

The scholarly response to *The Death of Jim Loney* has ranged from Peter Wild's assault on various features of it, his most important objection being his argument that the protagonist "is a pathetic rather than a tragic figure,"[30] to Robert Gish's assertion that Loney's is an "antiheroic albeit tragic destiny," and his reminder of "the paradox that it lies within the cathartic power of tragic literature . . . to affirm life."[31] Commenting on the "visionary bird" as a symbol of the "transcendent reality" Loney is seeking, Dexter Westrum concludes paradoxically that for Loney, "[t]he only way to survive is not to survive within the confusion of his pointless existence. His transcendence [in death] is his triumph."[32] Louis Owens, however, suggests that while Loney does make a choice to die "like a warrior," he is in fact adopting "the stance of the Indian as tragic hero, the inauthentic gothic imposition of European America upon the Native American"; that is, Loney's freedom of choice is co-opted, and he "simply remains victimized by the authoritative discourse that defines the utterance 'Indian.'"[33] Owens's reading of the novel clearly opposes those of scholars like Paula Gunn Allen, who sees Loney as a "questor" who obtains "a vision that becomes the guiding force in his life and his death."[34] Similarly, Kathleen Sands notes the importance of dreams and visions in Native American culture, concluding that Loney's death is "an honorable act that faces the impossibility of achieving connectedness in life."[35] David M. Craig, suggesting a parallel with Meursault in Camus's *The Stranger* argues that by choosing the place and circumstances of his death Loney affirms life and self, for death provides the "unity of experience for which he yearns; only death can provide a sense of self,"[36] and John Scheckter sees in the novel the "extreme difficulty," but the "absolute necessity, of maintaining a sense of individual dignity."[37]

Other aspects of the novel that have drawn particular attention are the theme of alienation (Craig, Allen); the appearance of Indian motifs, including the mysterious bird (Sands, Westrum, Bevis, Barry, In-the-Woods, Purdy); the function of landscape (Craig, Nelson); the failure of communication (Costa); and the roles of women (Wiget, McFarland, Antell). In addition to the possible motif of the vision quest, Nora Barry suggests that the Gros Ventre and Blackfeet tales of lost or abandoned children lend the novel "an elegiac rather than a despairing tone."[38] John Purdy associates the dark bird with "Bha'a or Thunderbird, Ruler of Storms."[39] David Craig perceives in the novel a "geography of aloneness" and argues that on the Montana Highline "the people's lives are equally distant" and that the physical nearness of the bars only emphasizes their "emotional distance" from each other,[40] while Robert Nelson offers an elaborate reading of the novel in which the east-west running Highline (US 2) would connect Loney with the white world of flight and diminished identity, while the south, which leads to the reservation and Mission Canyon, promises "complete reintegration of his life with the regenerative spirit of the land."[41] Rachel Barritt Costa's essay demonstrates what is perhaps obvious enough to any reader, that "this is a novel very much concerned with problems of language," particularly with the failure of Ike Loney to communicate with his son and with Jim Loney's inability to communicate with anyone.[42]

Welch's treatment of women in *Winter in the Blood* prompted Kenneth Lincoln to note parenthetically that "it is an under-
statement to say that feminist readers do not take to this book."[43]
Andrew Wiget asserts that Rhea and Kate "are cut from the same
emasculating mold as Welch's other women, the first a smother-
ing mother replacement, the second an intimidating competi-
tor."[44] But anyone who will take the time to survey the list of
scholars and critics who have written about Welch's novels will
quickly discover that at least half of them are women, including
Paula Gunn Allen, A. LaVonne Ruoff, Kathleen Sands, Nora
Barry, Kathryn Vangen, Patricia Riley In-the-Woods, and
Roberta Orlandini. Ron McFarland places Loney's "cold busi-
nesswoman" sister, Kate, against the stereotypes of both the "bar
woman" and the nurturing wife/mother/grandmother, and he
finds Loney's schoolteacher girlfriend, Rhea Davis, "virtually
sinister in her superficiality," concluding that "neither Rhea nor
Kate offers Jim Loney the comforts of hearth and home (or
lodge) or the reassurance of his masculinity which one might
conventionally associate with the female, whether Indian or
not."[45] Judith A. Antell examines the relationship between strong
Indian women and alienated males in several Native American
novels, including *The Death of Jim Loney,* in which she notes
that "the Indian mother of the past no longer exists, and the
Indian mother of the twentieth century is a truly disturbing figure."[46] As Antell observes, Loney is a "motherless child" who is
also separated from his sister, and in the important search-for-
mother motif, which echoes throughout the text, Loney searches
not only for information about his biological mother, but also for
the identity of Sandra, Ike's mistress and Loney's surrogate

mother for a short time. Rhea shows no maternal impulses to speak of, and in fact it would not be until his third novel, *Fools Crow,* that Welch would depict women positively in that role. Sylvester Yellow Calf's mother is also a missing person in Welch's fourth novel, *The Indian Lawyer,* as is his father, but he shows no interest in her, having accepted his grandmother as a surrogate.

Perhaps the fundamental issue with *The Death of Jim Loney* remains that which Peter Wild addressed just four years after the novel's publication: Does Loney's unusual death leave us "in the midst of melodrama," or does Welch attain, as Paula Gunn Allen suggests, "the tragic vision"?[47] The last half-dozen chapters of the novel are devoted to what in classic studies of the dramatic structure of tragedy would be called the "catastrophe." Jim Loney's tragedy stands at an even greater distance than Willy Loman's from the aristocratic mode defined by Aristotle and shaped around the concept of the fall of the great from high place. Loney's is proletarian tragedy, and his dreams, to the extent that he has any besides alcohol induced hallucinations, are never clearly articulated, but they amount to a dream of survival, a release from suffering. Typical of the ghetto-bound member of the lower class or underclass, Loney does not dream of success or conquest in the greater world, but is limited in his vision to the world of his immediate environs, so his dreams are even less impressive than those of Willy Loman, but the degree of his suffering, and of the commensurate catharsis for the reader, is not less because his dreams are diminished.

In common with all tragic protagonists, from Oedipus and Othello through Hamlet and Willy Loman, Jim Loney's driving desire is to be able to understand and accept himself; and one of the major differences between him and the others is that they seem to be, one might say almost blissfully, unaware of what they truly desire until it is too late. In this respect, at least, Loney's pain is greater than theirs: He is all too completely aware of what he desires. In all of these instances, as in most tragedies, the burden of the revealed self proves too much for the individual, and it is that, more than the tragic flaw of imprudent haste (the shooting of Myron Pretty Weasel), or the mysterious force of fate (perhaps symbolized by the dark bird), or the machinations of an evil Iago (the three bullies—Ike, Painter, and Quentin), that crushes this tragic hero/victim.

CHAPTER FIVE

The Epic Design of *Fools Crow*

As James Welch said in an interview with Joseph Bruchac, his third novel, *Fools Crow* (1986), presents "a much larger landscape than the other two novels and it shows where some of the younger characters in the first two books are coming from."[1] Already in that interview, published the year *Fools Crow* won the *Los Angeles Times* Book Award for Fiction, Welch was contemplating his next novel, *The Indian Lawyer* (1990), which was to deal with Indian life in an urban setting and was to draw on his ten years of service on the Montana State Board of Pardons (the parole board). *Fools Crow* is an historical novel set in northern Montana between the end of the Civil War and the Marias River Massacre that occurred in January of 1870 and ended the existence of the warlike Blackfeet as an autonomous and independent people. It is also a prose epic, comprising such features as focus on episodes of vital importance to the history of the nation or people, broad scope, direct intervention of the "gods," and characters of heroic proportions. From a Eurocentric viewpoint, Welch's may not be aptly described as a "high style," but an "answerable style," to appropriate the phrase Milton uses in his prologue to the ninth book of *Paradise Lost.* The protagonist in the novel, who first bears the rather undignified name White Man's Dog, but earns the new name Fools Crow, about 150 pages into the text, has a much clearer sense of himself and of his place in the world (his destiny) than the alienated protagonists of either of the first two novels. Presumably, this is because the tribe provides the foundation of his identity and the way for him to evolve into manhood. As John Purdy observes, early in the novel, on the horse raid against the Crow, "The search for identity becomes a group effort."[2] Whether White Man's Dog/Fools Crow achieves "heroic" stature may be debatable, but Robert Franklin Gish is not alone among those who have detected in the novel what he calls "an epic sweep."[3]

The Blackfeet mythology is intact in this novel, available only through visits to a distant tribal elder (old Yellow Calf, who turns out to be the narrator's grandfather in *Winter in the Blood*) or a mysterious and perhaps even hallucinatory dark bird (as in *The Death of Jim Loney*). The spirit world is close to the protagonist, and in some ways it is less surprising to see him converse casually with animals like the wolverine or the raven than it is to encounter his awareness of historical events and personalities. Like Aeneas, a more communal hero than the egocentric Achilles, Fools Crow senses that he and his people exist in a moment of crisis. And unlike the major characters of the two earlier novels, whose sense of life and the world beyond their postal code is sharply limited and solipsistic, Fools Crow and other members of the Pikuni (Piegan) Blackfeet are well aware of their perilous instant in time. The whites (Napikwans) threaten to extinguish every trace of the world as they know it, replacing the wild and universally available buffalo with Herefords, a jealously possessed commodity. The Blackfeet are also well aware, for example, of the significance of the white trader-turned-rancher Malcolm Clark, who has taken a Pikuni wife. The warrior Yellow Kidney takes pains to avoid the Napikwan town at Many-sharp-points-ground (Helena) because he knows the whites hate and fear the Indians, wish to exterminate them, and want "the blue-coated seizers" to gun them down so they can graze their "whitehorns," as opposed to "blackhorns" (buffalo).[4] While the narrator of *Winter in the Blood* and Jim Loney are locked up in personal problems that may be interpreted in some ways as "representative" of the dilemmas of colonization, or the alienation of the Native American by Anglo culture, or the predicament of the mixed-blood, Fools Crow's personal issues, which do exist and are fully integrated into the novel, are framed in a broader, and one cannot help thinking more profound, context.

It would be condescending to describe the world that Welch portrays here as either "idyllic" or "innocent." It is "primitive," not in the sense of "savage," but in the etymological sense of being "prime" or "primal." William Bevis points out that in this portrait of "the Indian's world before the buffalo went away," the reader is not given a "white man's date until page 284."[5] The qualifiers or adjectives one settles on are important here: The world of the Pikunis could be described as "simple" in an honorific, Thoreauvian sense, which implies neither "crude" nor "simplistic." Accordingly, the language they use, as Welch presents it in translated form (the linguistic term for the process is "calque," a sort of loan translation), is close to the bone. Consider, for example, the word "buffalo," which comes into English by way of Italian, Latin, and Greek (*boubalos* for buffalo or antelope, which is derived from *bous* for ox). The Pikuni simply call it "blackhorn" because its horns are black. Many of Welch's calques (like "sits-beside-him-wife," "many-shots gun," and "white-scabs disease") are drawn from the work of James Willard Schultz, who lived among the Blackfeet in the early 1880s.

Some of the linguistic features Welch imports for this novel would be readily understood by nearly any reader. White Man's Dog, for example, is described as being "eighteen winters" old (3), and he tells a friend he has been unlucky "for many moons" (7). Hollywood has more than adequately prepared readers for such "natural" time indicators. But from the first pages readers are confronted with a strange vocabulary that can seem awkward and forced and that may constitute the greatest risk Welch takes in the novel: skinned-tree houses and many-shots guns (4), ears-far-apart (5), wood-biter (6), big-leaf tree (7). Most of these locutions are obvious enough or are defined in their immediate context (the "ears-far-apart," for example, is hooting in the distance). Similarly, the neighboring tribes are given descriptive names instead of European ones, so the Cheyenne are "Spotted Horse People," the Nez Perce are "Black Paint People," and the Assiniboine are "Cutthroat People." The publishers provide a useful map of the area with these designations, so a reader needs only flip to the front of the novel to be reminded that the "Entrails People" are the Gros Ventres. Certainly, however, there are moments in the novel when some readers will wish Welch had provided a glossary for other such calques.

The effect on the reader of Welch's technique is somewhat similar to that in *For Whom the Bell Tolls,* in which Hemingway attempts to write dialogue in English as if the syntax and idiom were Spanish: [Robert Jordan] "Camarada to me is what all should be called with seriousness in this war. In the joking commences a rottenness." [Pilar] "Thou art very religious about thy politics."[6] Arguably, Welch has even better cause to invent an "answerable style" than his favorite novelist. As Gish describes it, Welch uses this linguistic technique in the process of "re-creating the world of the Lone Eaters" (the particular band of Pikunis to which Fools Crow belongs): "He invents his own scheme of naming which, whether real or an approximation, has the intended effect of establishing an older (but for the reader newer) way of knowing." Gish notes that "such naming can be frivolous" and that Welch does risk a certain "silliness" in his effort "to transport the reader back as far as the novel, written within its conventions and in English, will allow."[7] Bevis suggests that, in a way, the novel was "impossible to write. We cannot enter an alien world in a comfortable manner. . . . There is no diction that can simultaneously be easy, yet shock us with difference." But the result, Bevis concludes, "is an opportunity for us to come closer to the buffalo-culture Indian world than in any other novel to date."[8] With respect to Welch's manipulation of syntax and phrasing, Louis Owens observes that the tensions "within the very language of the novel become a radical indicator of the cultural denigration, displacement, even genocide that the novel is meant to demonstrate."[9] That is, the reader becomes acutely aware of the lost, or more accurately "eradicated," native language that Welch is trying to represent in English, the language of the conqueror and colonizer. As Owens suggests, "Writing in predominantly simple declarative sentences and avoiding complex syntactical constructions . . . while simultaneously avoiding the cliché formal pidgin of Hollywood Indians" is Welch's great stylistic challenge with this novel.[10]

Welch drew the names of his characters from various sources, including historical accounts and George Bird Grinnell's *Blackfoot Lodge Tales*.[11] The birth name of White Man's Dog is Sinopa, which Welch might have taken from Grinnell, who lists it as the band or society name of the kit-fox, which was thought to have the strongest medicine of them all.[12] Or Welch might have taken the name from the title character in a novel by James Willard Schultz, whose works he consulted in the process of writing *Fools Crow*.[13]

As the following, extended plot synopsis indicates, Welch is much more concerned in *Fools Crow* with action and event than in the two previous novels, which pivoted on the inner lives of the protagonists. The story begins in proper epic fashion, *in medias res,* as winter approaches the Pikuni camp of the Lone Eaters, and White Man's Dog, the former Sinopa, at age eighteen feels unlucky, as he has neither wives nor horses, his animal helper (wolverine) appears to be weak, and he has no feats of heroism to his credit (his younger brother, Running Fisher, at age sixteen, has taken two horses in raids). Although he prays to the Above Ones, White Man's Dog has the hero's consciousness that finding his own power, or coming into his manhood, is "up to him" (4). The reader also gets brief glimpses of White Man's Dog's father, Rides-at-the-door (age forty-seven), who is worried for his son, and of Kills-close-to-the-lake, his third and youngest wife (she is about seventeen years old), who appears to be interested romantically in White Man's Dog.

White Man's Dog's first opportunity to enter manhood comes when the warrior Yellow Kidney (aged thirty-eight) agrees to take him along with four other young men on a horse-stealing expedition against the Crow, a fifteen-day ride to the south. Welch defines the incongruity of the Blackfeet's world when he brackets Yellow Kidney's concerns about the whites, whose territorial capital at Helena they must avoid, with the dreams of the braggart,

Fast Horse, about which Yellow Kidney is skeptical, and of White Man's Dog, whose "steadiness" and "calmness" Yellow Kidney admires despite his bad luck (13–18). That is, the Blackfeet live in a world in which dreams and visions are as real as the coffee, sugar, and white man's water offered at the treaty talks on the Missouri River. As William Bevis observes, "Dreaming in this novel is exactly the opposite of dreaming in Freud. Instead of taking us deeper into psyche and individual variation, it takes us out of private psyche and into a public world."[14] Fast Horse tells Yellow Kidney about his dream of Cold Maker and a clogged ice spring, which augurs bad luck for the raid, but White Man's Dog does not tell his confusing dream of an enemy camp with naked, dead girls and a white-faced girl who beckons to him. They strike the large camp of Bull Shield, a Crow chief, and in the process White Man's Dog must kill a young brave who would otherwise have sounded an alarm (this kill does not establish his manhood). Readers watch Yellow Kidney approach the chief's tent as snow begins to fall, and that is the last they see of him for some time.

Of the epic heroes in Western literature, White Man's Dog most closely resembles the "pious Aeneas" of Virgil's epic, for his concerns tend away from individual heroic deeds and toward the welfare of the community (in this case, the tribe). White Man's Dog wonders why they are suffering, and he develops a liaison with seventy-four-year-old Mik-api, the powerful medicine man, who sends him on a mission that straddles the border between the real and the visionary world. To an extent this mission involves a vision quest and the discovery of a power animal which will help White Man's Dog define himself, but more important, his individual or personal power will be employed for the benefit of the tribe in the coming hard times.

One appealing attribute of the novel is the deftness with which Welch handles such border-crossings between the mundane and the spiritual, the effect of which on the reader is similar to that of magic realist fiction in the vein of Gabriel García Márquez, Luisa Valenzuela, and other Latin American writers. Mik-api tells White Man's Dog that Raven has appeared to him in a dream and asked him to send his helper to free Skunk Bear (Wolverine) from a white man's trap. White Man's Dog follows Raven's advice, frees the animal (presumably in the "real" world), and is commended by Raven (presumably from the "visionary" or "magic" world): "Of all the two-leggeds, you alone will possess the magic of Skunk Bear. You will fear nothing, and you will have many horses and wives. But you must not abuse this power, and you must listen to Mik-api, for I speak through him."(58). Raven and Wolverine communicate directly and sometimes rather playfully with White Man's Dog in a manner reminiscent of that with which Athena speaks with Odysseus or Venus with Aeneas, but with greater intimacy and familiarity. Along with these visionary animals, Mik-Api will see to it that White Man's Dog's powers work for the benefit of the tribe.

As spring approaches, the renegade Owl Child, of the Many Chiefs band, appears at the Lone Eaters camp with horses he has stolen from the whites, but he is turned away. Fast Horse, whom several critics have described as a "foil" character for Fools Crow, runs off to join Owl Child when Yellow Kidney appears, his fingers having been cut off after he was captured by the Crow.[15] Yellow Kidney tells how Fast

Horse's loud, boastful cry gave him away during the raid and how he hid in what turned out to be a death lodge, where he copulated with a girl dying of smallpox. Yellow Kidney was saved by the Cheyenne, but he is burdened with shame and is unable to support his family. White Man's Dog now recognizes the significance of his dream, and struggling with guilt for not having told the others about it, he commits himself to hunting for Yellow Kidney's family. Rides-at-the-door tells his son the disaster occurred because the world is "out of balance" (85), and he blames Fast Horse. When White Man's Dog is chosen to spread the news of the Sun Dance to other Pikuni bands, his brother, Running Fisher, whom John Purdy associates with Fast Horse as a character "moved by self-interest rather than communal,"[16] becomes envious. Power is lost, Purdy notes, when "immediate and transitory concerns of the individual" subvert "a sense of selfless devotion to the best interests of the larger self: the community and its landscape."[17]

In Chapter Ten, the longest in the novel at twenty-seven pages, Welch details the mythology behind the Sun Dance and describes the ordeal of White Man's Dog, whose pain secures for him both the status of manhood, as recognized by the medicine man, Mik-api (117), and the full power of Wolverine, his spirit animal, with whom he converses in a dream, which takes place in a world of "glittering whiteness" (118). White Man's Dog marries Yellow Kidney's daughter, Red Paint (she bears the same name as Welch's Blackfeet great grandmother). At the end of the first part, Mountain Chief calls for peace with the whites, but Owl Child and his band, including Fast Horse, who have not attended the Sun Dance ceremony, ride away in anger.

Part 2 of the novel opens with Red Paint's announcement that she is pregnant and that their son will be called Sleep-bringer because of the butterfly she saw when she became aware of her condition. In a raid against the Crow to retaliate for what they did to Yellow Kidney, White Man's Dog acquits himself well. After he is wounded and falls from his horse, White Man's Dog regains consciousness in time to shoot Bull Shield, and Rides-at-the-door proudly pronounces his son a "brave" (147). In the thirteenth chapter, a little more than a third of the way through the novel, White Man's Dog acquires his new name, Fools Crow, because he is thought to have intentionally tricked Bull Shield. Consequently, the newly named warrior feels there is a "bad spirit" in the world making him do "evil things," which includes his boasting to Yellow Kidney: "He had belittled his father-in-law without thinking, and he knew Yellow Kidney had lost face forever" (153). To make matters worse, a cavalry column arrives in camp with the news that Owl Child and his gang have murdered the rancher, Malcolm Clark. To the Pikuni, the fact that the soldiers are pursuing Mountain Chief is "like shooting one gopher because another gopher had bitten a child's finger" (159). This proverbial analogy might be said to echo not only through the rest of the novel, but also throughout the history of white treatment of Indians.

Feeling that war with the Napikwans is becoming unavoidable, Fools Crow and his wife find brief respite hunting in the Rockies as autumn begins. In a lengthy dialogue with Raven, who recounts the Blackfeet creation story, Fools Crow is told of "an evil presence here in the Backbone" (Rocky Mountains), a white hunter who kills animals indiscriminately and leaves the carcasses to rot (163). As is often the case in the epic genre, the hero is assigned the task of ridding the land of a powerful intruder. Raven helps Fools Crow by sending the Napikwan an erotic dream of a young Pikuni woman, and the next day Fools Crow waits for the hunter to be drawn to Red Paint, who is unaware that she is the bait for his trap. In a tense scene, Fools Crow is wounded, but manages to dispatch the sinister white man who wears a wolfskin headdress and, with his buckskins and bushy hair and beard, looks "like a molting blackhorn bull" (169). In effect, Fools Crow has succeeded in two epic combats, one with a powerful Indian adversary, Bull Shield, and another with the implicitly monstrous white man. Although Fools Crow's motives for killing the hunter are clearly honorable, and even praiseworthy given the circumstances, he has now taken a step toward the dreaded and apparently inevitable confrontation in which classical epics are usually resolved.

In the last two chapters of part 2, winter approaches and Fast Horse, who has been Fools Crow's boyhood friend, appears at the camp severely wounded. Although Mik-api, with Fools Crow's assistance, cures the rebellious brave, Fast Horse can no longer accept the beliefs and values of his tribe, even though his father, Boss Ribs, is keeper of the Beaver Medicine bundle, the symbolic power source of the Pikuni. As part 3 opens, we encounter Owl Child with Fast Horse and others about to raid a ranch, but the scene shifts suddenly to Fools Crow, as he follows them in what he knows will be the vain hope of convincing Fast Horse to return. Away from the tribe and apart from his wife and parents, Fools Crow briefly experiences the giddy "freedom of being alone," but he instantly reminds himself that "this freedom from responsibility, from accountability to the group" is selfish and will mean suffering for the Pikuni, and "his own feeling of freedom deserted him" (211). Some readers will find this distinctively "modern" thought process, and similar moments in the novel, to be incongruous, and perhaps unconvincing. Fools Crow's perspective, however, is to be distinguished from that of such heroes as Achilles, or even Odysseus. Fools Crow emerges as a paternal figure even though he is a young man, and he is also set apart from Fast Horse (and from such heroic figures as Beowulf) by his humility. Like Aeneas, who denies his own love for Dido, Fools Crow rejects personal freedom for the good of the tribe.

In the final scene of Chapter Eighteen, Owl Child and his band viciously attack the ranch and almost inevitably alienate the reader from any sympathy for their cause. In the next chapter, which serves as dramatic relief, Double Strike Woman, Fools Crow's mother, reflects on her son's evolution from his identity as Sinopa, to White Man's Dog (so named because when he was nine he followed after the old storyteller, Victory Robe White Man), to Fools Crow, and she thinks bitterly of Fast Horse and "that whole gang of killers he ran with" (218). In effect, Welch makes certain that the reader turns against the renegade band. The reader also observes Double Strike Woman's positive response to the plural marriage system followed by the Blackfeet and some other Plains Indians, but the chapter ends with the betrayal of that custom when Kills-close-to-the-lake, Rides-at-the-door's youngest wife at age eighteen, commits adultery with Fools Crow's brother, Running Fisher.

Welch's description of the sex act is couched in the diction of the harlequin romance: "With a shudder she pulled him down and felt his warmth growing against her thigh. . . . At that moment he was everything she possessed in the world, and she gave herself to him" (224). The questions posed for the reader by such a passage are whether the writer is intentionally echoing the hackneyed mode of the pulp romance, and if so, why or to what end? If this were Welch's first novel, such a passage would almost certainly have drawn critical fire, but given his maturity as a novelist, it is almost impossible to think that the echoes are unintended. What he accomplishes here is an implicit critique of what might be called the primitive idyll. Welch is not writing melodrama in which the villainous whites are arrayed against the virtuous and noble Redman. Betrayal of family and tribe on the disastrous level of Owl Child and Fast Horse is, in effect, mirrored on a lesser scale in this betrayal on a more personal and intimate level. The cliché language renders the act banal and repugnant, and being Indian even in the days before the white conquest, Welch implies, did not necessarily mean being morally pure. The "nobility" of the Indian is no less of a stereotype than the "savagery." Welch insists that his Native Americans be human.

In the chapter that follows, Fools Crow catches up with Fast Horse, but fails to convince him to return to the tribe. Fast Horse connects his apostasy with the strange dream of Cold Maker and the hidden ice spring, which he had prior to the ill-fated raid on the Crow camp, and Welch constructs the chapter so that between Fools Crow's pursuit and the final meeting, we see Yellow Kidney, who regards himself as a "near-man" (230), leaving the Lone Eaters camp for the land of the Cheyenne. That is, we are reminded of the cost to others of Fast Horse's self-centeredness. While Owl Child's raid on the Standley ranch involves vengeance and intentional violence, the killing of Yellow Kidney, who decides to return to his family, exemplifies an almost accidental kind of violence that contributes to the growing sense of inevitable tragedy. A white man and his son come upon the shelter where Yellow Kidney is spending the night, and fueled with the story of "what they did to Frank Standley and his wife," he is ready to shoot the first Indian he comes upon (242). Among Yellow Kidney's final thoughts is the grandson he will never meet, but whom he would like to name Yellow Calf, "a strong name, one that would someday be spoken with fear in the camps of the enemies" (245). As Robert Franklin Gish has observed, this Yellow Calf is at least nominally associated with the old hunter who appears in *Winter in the Blood,* and he appears once again in Welch's next novel, *Indian Lawyer,* in the surname of the protagonist, Sylvester Yellow Calf.[18]

In a council meeting that evening, the Lone Eaters chief Three Bears portrays the position of his band and others among the Pikunis as somewhere between that of Mountain Chief, whose band includes Owl Child, and Heavy Runner, who seeks to appease the whites at all costs: "They are as different as the real-bear [grizzly] and the prairie chicken" (254). But he makes it clear that he will go to war before aligning his band with that of Heavy Runner. As some readers (but probably not the majority) may know, it is Heavy Runner's band that will be destroyed in the upcoming "Massacre on the Marias," so this episode constitutes a sort of ironic foreshadowing.

As the catastrophic event approaches, Welch oscillates with increasing regularity between what might be called "domestic" and "historic" episodes. The rhythm is somewhat reminiscent of that in *War and Peace,* and as in Tolstoy's epic novel, the closer the moment of impending doom, the more precious are the episodes of domestic life. This is not to say, however, that the episodes involving the domestic life of the tribe are bland or without drama. In Chapter Twenty-three, for example, a young Pikuni boy is attacked by a wolf, and with Mik-api at another village, Fools Crow must summon all he has learned about medicine and magic to cure him. In the process, Fools Crow confirms his new identity as a healer. Part 3 then ends with a meeting on the Milk River between several Pikuni and Kainah chiefs and General Alfred H. Sully, whose views on the Indian situation are regarded as moderate (as was the case historically). Welch treats Sully sympathetically, but the demands he must make of the Blackfeet, which include the surrender of Owl Child and return of stolen livestock, are obviously beyond their capacity to satisfy. As Rides-at-the-door contemplates the fact that "their choices were ending" (284), Heavy Runner and three other chiefs request documents that indicate they are "not to be considered hostile." Even those readers who do not know the story of the Marias River Massacre are likely to detect the ironic foreshadowing at this point.

Part 4 begins with a powerful episode which, like many in Welch's novels, can stand by itself and which makes his fiction suitable for anthologies even though he does not write short stories. A former Confederate cavalry officer, a deserter from Georgia who is guarding whiskey wagons on their way to Canada, is killed by Fast Horse. But what gives the episode its impact is the deftness and vividness with which Welch creates the minor character and endows him with a life-story: "They had just finished planting the first crop of cotton and were eating a big supper complete with a bottle of French wine his father had saved for the occasion when a Negro from Parnell's place rode into the yard on a mule and shouted that war had broken out" (292). In his last moments, "He thought about the thick stands of pine in Georgia," "his sisters would be grown now," and he longs to be "sitting down to a meal of biscuits and gravy" (293). Then Welch demolishes the unnamed man's domestic dreams by having him killed while he is urinating. The episode is not gratuitous, nor does it simply exist to undercut potential sympathy for an Anglo character, for it is in the context of this raid, carried out close to some Pikuni camps, that both Fast Horse and Owl Child realize they have endangered their people and that their own time is running out as well.

From that episode the pendulum swings back to the domestic life of the Lone Eaters as a white doctor brings a warning of a smallpox epidemic, Fast Horse discovers Yellow Kidney's body in the deserted war lodge, and a council of the Lone Eaters struggles to decide whether they should turn their backs on fellow Pikunis and move to Canada to avoid the disease, as the white doctor has advised. The impending crisis strikes at the very heart of the tribe, undermining the guiding principles of community. At this crucial moment, Fools Crow falls into a sleep, in which he is approached by Nitsokan, dream helper.

The remaining five chapters of part 4 constitute a sort of parallel to the sixth book of *The Aeneid,* in which the hero enters the Underworld in order to acquire prophecy. This kind of episode has been recognized as one of the fundamental conventions of epic literature, but in *Fools Crow* the journey is not into a nether region, but into a "green sanctuary between earth and sky" (360). Fools Crow's quest requires self-humiliation and self-abnegation. He paints himself in white, a sort of death-mask, and he travels alone as a beggar, depriving himself of either food or rest. Welch constructs the episode in an oscillatory fashion, interrupting his initial entrance into a hidden canyon blocked by a boulder (an obvious reference to Fast Horse's dream of the blocked ice spring) and his meeting with a mysterious woman dressed in white with a short chapter in which Fast Horse, now having left Owl Child's gang, returns Yellow Kidney's body to the Lone Eaters. In the next chapter Fools Crow watches the strange woman paint a design on a yellow skin, but when he awakens, the design has disappeared and the woman, who now looks younger, is digging turnips. Readers familiar with Plains Indian mythology will readily recognize her as Feather Woman, So-at-sa-ki, whose legend is recounted in the last chapter of part 4, after an intervening chapter returns us to the domestic, real-world, where Rides-at-the-door is compelled to banish his third wife, Kills-close-to-the-lake, and his younger son, Running Fisher, for their adultery, which has brought dishonor to the family. As in nearly all heroic societies, that of the Blackfeet is a shame-culture, in which "honor is all we have" (339). The additional possession of the Blackfeet is the buffalo, but as Rides-at-the-door reflects, "Take away one or the other and we have nothing. One feeds us and the other nourishes us" (339–40).

Feather Woman identifies herself in answer to Fools Crow's question, "Why do you mourn?" (349) She mourns the loss of her husband, Morning Star, and of her son, Star Boy or Poia (also known as Scar Face). She tells Fools Crow of how she dug out the sacred turnip, which she was forbidden to do, and how that left a hole in the sky, which brought both her banishment from the heavens, and misery and suffering to the human world below. Some readers will detect parallels between Feather Woman's mythic role and that of Eve in Judeo-Christian lore. Fools Crow points out that she should take pride in having given birth to Poia, who taught the Pikunis the Sun Dance ceremony, which involves ritual self-torture reminiscent of traditional Christian penitential rites. Feather Woman unrolls the yellow skin and causes the prophetic design to come to life, revealing a smallpox epidemic, the attack of the seizers, and the disappearance of the buffalo and consequent starvation of the Blackfeet. At the end, Fools Crow sees Napikwan "children, running and playing, laughing" while dark-skinned children stand to the side and a large white woman holds a brass bell (358). Unlike such epic heroes as Aeneas, it will not be Fools Crow's role to conquer the enemy, but to prepare the people "for the times to come." "If they make peace within themselves," Feather Woman advises, "they will live a good life in the Sand Hills [the afterlife]. There they will go on to live as they always have" (359).

The fifth and final part of the novel runs only about twenty-five pages and recounts the smallpox epidemic among the Lone Eaters and Fools Crow's discovery of the destruction of Heavy Runner's band by the cavalry on the Marias River. At the site of the massacre where soldiers killed 173 Indians on January 23, 1870,[19] Black Prairie Runner, one of the survivors, laments, "This world has changed and we do not belong to it. . . . We would rather be killed by the Napikwans than live in their world" (385). But Welch decides against concluding the novel with such a coldly realistic outlook, offering instead a final scene that functions as a surprisingly optimistic epilogue, reminiscent of the one from *Winter in the Blood*. He portrays the aging Mik-api, who has chosen Fools Crow as his successor, leading the survivors in a spring dance watched over by Fools Crow, Red Paint, and their newborn son, Butterfly. Fools Crow feels "a peculiar kind of happiness—a happiness that sleeps with sadness," and he also feels an awareness of himself "removed from the others, dancing alone" because he is "burdened with the knowledge of his people" who, despite the changes in their lives, will survive (390), partly because Fools Crow (like Welch) is a storyteller and has assured that their stories will endure. The last image Welch impresses on the reader's mind is that of buffalo, great herds returning, "and, all around, it was as it should be" (391).

Robert Franklin Gish suggests that the novel implies "allegorical interpretations of not just the survival of the Blackfeet at the dawn of the twentieth century, but of the problematic survival of humanity, and even the biosphere."[20] Louis Owens describes the conclusion as "a lyrical—almost Homeric—vision."[21] For many readers, however, the lyric optimism of the ending will be darkly compromised by their awareness of historical reality, and for those who have read Welch's earlier novels, the pains of survival may be more evident than the gains. After all, Fools Crow's vision of the Pikunis' future also includes "a vast, empty prairie" devoid of buffalo (356). One critic describes the last scene as "ominously pastoral," detecting in Welch's "happiness that sleeps with sadness" the bittersweet melancholia of Keats's odes.[22]

William W. Bevis surmises that Welch attempted the "historical epic" because he thought it was important for the Blackfeet "to know how they had once lived and how they had come to their present life."[23] He adds that this perspective does imply "moral purpose," and that in various ways, including its resistance to "psychology," *Fools Crow* is not a "modern" novel (821). Bevis concludes that in the world depicted by Welch in this novel, "What matters is how they have acted and whether they can bear with dignity and honor the consequences of their actions" (822). That kind of value system is implicit in epic literature. Nora Barry detects in Fools Crow "a new kind of culture hero" whose battles will not be against mythological monsters or human warriors like Hector or Turnus, but a hero whose battlefields will be those "of the human spirit." She concludes that the "true historicity of this novel resides in its presentation of the Blackfeet way of life and in its redefinition of Blackfeet heroism in epic terms."[24]

CHAPTER SIX

Going One-on-One
The Indian Lawyer as Novel of Intrigue

If *The Death of Jim Loney* can be regarded as a sort of antitype of *Winter in the Blood, The Indian Lawyer* (1990), Welch's fourth novel, might be said to be the antitype, perhaps even the complement, of *Fools Crow*. The protagonist, Sylvester Yellow Calf, is introduced as a lawyer who is more or less coincidentally a Blackfeet Indian working for an influential firm in Helena, the state capital of Montana, but by the end of the book he is a lawyer who deals particularly with tribal litigation for the Sioux at the Standing Rock reservation in North Dakota. That is, he evolves from being a lawyer who happens to be Indian to a lawyer who deals with Indian-related issues, and is therefore an "Indian lawyer" in the full sense of the term. In some ways, as Welch suggests on a couple of occasions near the end of the novel, this change in directions constitutes a "fall from grace,"[1] but most readers will concur that in resigning his place on the state parole board and giving up his run for a seat in Congress on the Democratic ticket, Sylvester saves himself and begins the revival and regeneration of his character. Whether this process involves embracing his "Indianness," however, is problematic.

Like his first three novels, *The Indian Lawyer* is first of all a "novel of character"; that is, Welch customarily focuses the reader's attention on the protagonist's psychological or spiritual evolution or (in some cases) his transformation. In the case of *Fools Crow,* the title character undergoes a transformation so explicit and so powerful that his name changes (from White Man's Dog to Fools Crow). The unnamed protagonist-narrator of *Winter in the Blood,* a highly episodic novel with strong elements of the picaresque, experiences relatively little alteration, although he does appear to have thawed the metaphoric winter within and to have come to terms with his repressed past. Jim Loney, the title character of Welch's second novel, may be said to manifest less change than the protagonists of the other novels, which is what one might predict for a "tragic hero." While he does make important discoveries about himself, Loney is no more able to alter his destiny than Oedipus or Othello. Novels of character tend to deal particularly with the theme of self-identity as the protagonist strives to discover what sort of person he or she is, what matters most to him or her in life, and ultimately, what that life will mean.

The Indian Lawyer is Welch's most straightforward novel in several ways, and that makes it for some readers his most readily accessible. In it we encounter neither the mysterious dreams and visions of *Fools Crow,* nor the surreal leaps in logic and flashes of absurdity of *Winter in the Blood.* Structurally, as the plot summary will attest, the novel is linear and conventional, and it is divided into sixteen chapters, which run from nine to thirty-two pages; that is, readers do not encounter four or five parts with multi-chapter subdivisions, nor do they find the one- or two-page chapters that function as transitions or as lyrical intermezzos. In effect, the impact of this novel differs considerably from that of his earlier work, but whether that is all to the good depends on the reader. While one reviewer commended the "well-crafted plot," another argued that the "very serious idea" about which Welch has written "is all but lost in the banality of his plot."[2] David Seals, a member of the Huron tribe and author of *The Powwow Highway* (1979), which became a cult classic when it was made into a movie in 1989, argued in a lengthy review essay published in the *Nation* that "polished prose is not where 'Indian literature' comes from."[3] Seals, whose antagonism may owe something to his inability to find a large commercial publisher for his first novel, described *The Indian Lawyer* as "slick and sympathetic, just like the main character."[4] Lee Lemon complained that Welch's portrayal of the problems of being Native American in white society "are as predictable and as unexciting as the action."[5] Edward Hoagland, however, found the novel to be "Welch's most mature and readable book" to date, and William Hoagland, after commending the characterization, concluded, "At his best, Welch rises to lyrical description infused with psychological luminosity."[6]

Stylistically, *The Indian Lawyer* offers greater range than the earlier novels. Probably because several of the characters represent the criminal underclass of society, the writing at times reads like that of the popular thriller or melodrama, as in the rhetorical questions that Patti Ann, the wife of a convict, poses to herself about adoption: "What would it hurt? Mightn't it bring some happiness to them to start life anew with a child they could both love? Was that asking too much?" (95) If such writing strikes some readers as banal, it is most likely because Welch intends for the sentiments and their expression to match the character. Sylvester Yellow

Calf, the Indian lawyer, is generally connected with a vocabulary and an esthetic and social perspective more in line with his education and vocation, as in the following passage, which concerns the case through which he meets his Anglo girlfriend, Shelley Hatton Browers: "Sylvester's role in selling off the two ranches was enhanced by the fact that although there were several bidders lined up he found another buyer for one of them, a conservancy group that bought up land to protect flora and fauna that would otherwise be endangered" (115). Predictably, the most lyrical passages are those pertaining to the Montana landscape, as in the following, where Sylvester drives along the basin of the Prickly Pear Valley and reflects on the forest fire that is mentioned, perhaps with symbolic overtones of danger and devastation, throughout the first two-thirds of the novel: "A rainbow glimmered faintly beneath it, mostly yellow and green. And the foothills were unnaturally golden in the evening sun. Then Sylvester saw the column of smoke to the southeast. It was a soft, puffy cloud above the dark mountains, blowing in no particular direction. A dusty volatility hung in the air over the valley" (39). Evidence of his genesis as a poet may be detected throughout his fiction, but as various critics have observed over the years, Welch is a master of the plain-style, "flat and quiet, . . . tacit and understated."[7]

    In both *Fools Crow* and *The Indian Lawyer,* Welch's fundamental device for constructing plot (it is not especially innovative) is oscillation, the pendulum-like swinging back and forth between settings and characters. The technique allows him to play characters and settings against each other, sometimes with ironic impact, at other times with what might be called a tempering or balancing effect. Although he employed the technique occasionally in the two earlier novels, it has become more prevalent in the third and fourth, probably because the protagonists are not loners like the unnamed narrator of *Winter in the Blood* and Jim Loney. In both *Fools Crow* and *The Indian Lawyer,* secondary characters are more fully developed and have greater autonomy or individual identity than in the earlier novels; that is, their identity is not so fully dependent on that of the protagonists. In this respect in particular, Welch has demonstrated his maturity as a novelist

The novel opens not from the perspective of the title character, but from that of his antagonist, a thirty-five-year-old convict named Jack Harwood, who is different from the other inmates of the Montana state penitentiary at Deer Lodge because he has a college education. In effect, his status as a sort of "outsider" within the system inaugurates one of the most important thematic strands in the novel, for Sylvester Yellow Calf is himself an "outsider," both to his family and tribe, and to the world of the urban lawyer, in which he is in the process of becoming an "insider." As Sidner J. Larson has observed, "Because he has allowed himself to become an outsider to family, landscape, and tribal identity, Yellow Calf is poorly equipped to cope with challenges that arise."[8] Yellow Calf, like Welch, who served on the Montana Board of Pardons for ten years, serves on the board that denies Harwood's parole. Harwood is doing "his second stretch for armed robbery" (16), but Welch carefully builds some (albeit limited) reader sympathy for him by portraying him as the victim of a knifing by Indian inmates and by associating him with Patti Ann, his wife of nine years (seven of which he has spent behind bars). Readers also learn that Harwood used proceeds from one of his robberies to pay for his wife's hysterectomy. The Indians, who are outsiders in white society, are insiders in prison, whereas Harwood, who at least has the potential to be an insider in white society, is an outsider in prison. Welch does not portray the Indian inmates any more sympathetically than he does the Anglos.

At the end of the first chapter readers meet Patti Ann Harwood, who feels oddly relieved to learn that her husband has been denied parole, and when he urges her to flirt with Sylvester, in order to pressure him into supporting Jack's bid for parole, readers lose most of their sympathy for her husband. The second chapter implicitly plays the thirty-five-year-old attorney, who came from a broken family and grew up in the tough reservation town of Browning, but overcame the handicaps to become a basketball star at the University of Montana and go on to law school at Stanford, against Jack Harwood, who "came from a good family" and "had a normal childhood" (16), but wasted his opportunities. In common with all of his main characters but Fools Crow, Sylvester Yellow Calf's family is incomplete. The father of the unnamed narrator of *Winter in the Blood* is dead, and Jim Loney's mother has disappeared. Sylvester Yellow Calf is missing both parents, his mother a barfly and his father a wino (104), both of them having deserted him and left him in the care of his grandparents. Yellow Calf's mother joins several other hard "bar women" who desert their families in Welch's novels, and through Sylvester, Welch provides his harshest judgment: "Gradually he came to hate her too [as he hated his father] and imagined that she was dead, wished that she was dead" (250).

Sylvester's grandfather, Earl Yellow Calf, who has suffered a stroke, has rejected traditional tribal ways, but his grandmother, Little Bird Walking Woman (also known as Mary Bird), at eighty-seven, still goes to powwows and other tribal events. Although Sylvester has essentially turned away from his tribal roots, he is not fully at ease in the upscale world of Helena, with its dress-up social events and political machinations. One critic has connected Yellow Calf with N. Scott Momaday's Locke Setman from *Ancient Child* (1989), whom he describes as "the first, real, honest-to-God yuppie protagonist in Indian fiction."[9] But from the outset Sylvester experiences "a familiar feeling of unease" (38) and a "familiar discomfort" (48) when he finds himself among the political big shots who hope to make inroads into George Bush and the Republican party in the coming 1990 elections. To some extent, *The Indian Lawyer,* which takes place in the present, in the fall and winter of 1988–89, like *Fools Crow,* could be called an historical novel, and the same can be said of Welch's forthcoming novel, titled *The Heartsong of Charging Elk.* Neither of the first two novels could be so described.

Just as Sylvester Yellow Calf is played off against Jack Harwood, so is his blond, Anglo girlfriend Shelley, a thirty-three-year-old divorced mother of two daughters with a degree from Swarthmore and graduate work at the University of Pennsylvania, the antitype of the twice-married, auburn-haired beauty, Patti Ann, who has suffered four miscarriages and an hysterectomy. Sidner Larson observes that "Yellow Calf's relationships with his mother and grandmother have made him at once wary and appreciative of the attentions of women,"[10] and certainly those relationships constitute one set of keys to his character. Larson notes that because "women provided leadership in the shattered tribal culture of his youth," Sylvester turns to them "instinctively" when he is troubled.[11] Chapter Two ends with Yellow Calf explaining his altruistic and commendable rationale for agreeing to run for Congress. He identifies his own boyhood with that of a ragged, seven- or eight-year-old Indian boy he recalls having seen "playing marbles all by himself" (59). The illustrative tale is so reminiscent of the rhetorical strategies employed by actual politicians on the campaign trail that it may ring false to the reader, who may wonder whether Sylvester has fallen for his own hokey story. Presumably, readers have just witnessed a genuine and touching self-revelation, but the tale is so pat that it may cause some to suspect the depth of the protagonist's self-awareness. Shelley responds, predictably, by agreeing that as a member of Congress, he "can help that child and more just like him," and she adds that he is indeed "a good man" (60). As if to confirm that designation and simultaneously to prove his domesticity, Sylvester offers to fix omelets for them.

The sentimentality at the end of the second chapter is most likely intentional on Welch's part, as it sets up the reader for Patti Ann's seduction of Sylvester, which begins in the next chapter. In one of several clever echoes that resound throughout the novel, Patti Ann leaves Sylvester's office feeling "alive, free as a bird, a woman" (75). Careful readers will most likely recall the Indian name of Sylvester's grandmother, Little Bird Walking Woman (48). When Sylvester hangs up the phone after talking with Shelly, just after Patti Ann has left, he tells her, "'Love you too.' But the phone was dead" (78). Near the end of the next chapter, which shifts the focus to Jack Harwood in prison, the manipulative convict ends his phone call, which is laced with intimations of his eventual demand that his wife prostitute herself in order to set up his blackmail scheme, by saying, "Good girl. Love ya," to which Patti Ann responds, "'I love you too. . . .' But he had hung up" (93). In effect, the two distinct "worlds" around which the novel is constructed seem very far apart, but Welch implies that they are not so distant as one might think, and the reader becomes increasingly aware that those worlds will collide.

Chapter Five opens with Sylvester and Shelley in bed after a swim at a hot springs resort. Sylvester remembers fouling out of a basketball game against Boise State University, after which he recalls an episode during his high school days, when a sportswriter praised him as "the heart and soul of the greatest Indian basketball team this state has seen" (102). But being singled out from his teammates caused a distance to grow between himself and the others in the tribal community. As one critic suggests, "the more successful he becomes at basketball and beyond, and the more recognition he receives for his achievements, the further he distances himself from his people and his heritage," and eventually Sylvester finds that he has been led into "a spiritual cul-de-sac."[12] References to basketball recur frequently enough in the novel for readers to presume that the game acquires symbolic status. Ironically, it is the team sport played in "the way of good Indian teams" as "racehorse basketball" (100) that definitively sets Yellow Calf apart from the tribal community, but the reader should remember that, like old Yellow Calf, the Blackfeet warrior in *Winter in the Blood* who defied tribal custom by hunting for the Gros Ventre widow of Standing Bear, Sylvester has always been "different, even back there on the reservation" (38). In this respect in particular, that is, in his independence and his self-identity that is connected with but distinct from the family, tribe, and community, Sylvester Yellow Calf as a character is akin to the unnamed narrator, Jim Loney, and even to Fools Crow, who remains the protagonist most closely integrated with family-tribe-community.

In the fifth chapter Sylvester also reflects on various women who have been important to him, notably the school counselor, Lena Old Horn, who is just six years his senior, and who, because she is a Crow living on the Blackfeet reservation, is quite conscious of being an outsider. After the state basketball tournament and the sports feature, Sylvester's awareness that he "had always been a little different" (110) increases when he develops a crush on Lena, but Welch describes his infatuation as the "way that a youth falls in love with a special aunt" (111). Significantly, perhaps, he envisions Lena dressed "in buckskins and shawl doing beadwork or dancing a grass dance" (111), and in a one-on-one game of basketball with her white lover and fellow teacher, Sylvester seems deliberately to break the man's nose. Just how much one should make of such an episode is debatable. It could well be that Sylvester's hatred of Stanley Weintraub, an English teacher who encourages him to write, is a subconscious lashing out at the oppressive white world that he paradoxically both desires and dislikes. It is the world that has ruined his culture, but it is also the world from which he seeks confirmation of his identity.

Welch carefully moves back and forth between references to the present scene, with Shelley at the hot springs resort, and the remembered past. Consider the ironic juxtaposition, for example, when, after driving the teacher to the hospital, Sylvester eats "deer-meat stew and frybread" while his grandparents watch television (113), while on the next page he eats shrimp and breadsticks with Shelley. After Sylvester reflects on his relationship with Shelley, he recalls an intensely sexual affair with a woman from the Laguna Pueblo when he was at Stanford, a relationship that left him feeling an inexplicable "ambivalence" (128). Still uncertain as to whether he should announce for Congress, Sylvester recognizes that "he had always chosen women who put up barriers, either consciously or unconsciously, between themselves and happiness. And he further understood that he had done the same" (128). By the end of the chapter, it is obvious that his relationship with Shelley, which is reminiscent in some ways of Jim Loney's with Rhea, is doomed.

Against the present and remembered romances of Sylvester Yellow Calf, Welch plays off the brutality of Jack Harwood's life in prison in Chapter Six. There, he is beaten by Indian inmates who correctly suspect he has held out some money from one of the robberies (the money with which he paid for his wife's hysterectomy), and he is always aware of the dangers of sexual perversion, homosexual rape being chief among them. Although the language of the prison scenes is predictably crude, William Bevis has noted that "several high-school teachers in central Montana already use this rather racy and gritty book with advanced students because it is the only portrait in print of a successful, professional Native of their region."[13] In the next chapter Welch signals Patti Ann's approaching seduction of Sylvester with another echoic passage: "Somehow, a barrier had been pulled down, almost without assistance from either of them" (148).

In Chapter Eight Sylvester drives north to the Blackfeet reservation, well aware that although he "couldn't believe what had happened," he "knew that he had wanted it" (159), and he also realizes that Patti Ann has seduced him. He does not recognize her name (she calls herself Lowery), and he thinks he is in love. In one of the more painful scenes in the novel, the narrative focus shifts to Sylvester's grandmother, who recalls having given Sylvester her grandfather's sacred medicine pouch before he left for college, only to find it a week later "tucked behind some books" (162). The symbolism of his gesture is obvious. The medicine pouch, which is reminiscent of the one the protagonist of *Winter in the Blood* throws into the grave of his grandmother, had protected Mary Bird's warrior grandfather when he rode into battle. Sylvester's callous disregard of the gift, along with his subordination of it to the books that represent the Anglo world, casts his character in an even darker shadow, in some ways, than his sexual misconduct with Patti Ann.

While he admits that having a sexual relationship with a client is "stupid" (161), Yellow Calf demonstrates neither sensitivity nor understanding when it comes to the pouch, which he finds in his dresser. He holds it up to his neck in front of the mirror and tries to visualize a Blackfeet warrior going on a raid against the Crow, but all he sees is "a man with circles under his eyes, . . . a man whose only war, skirmish, actually, was with himself" (168). He sees now that he is not one of the so-called "new warriors," but "a fat cat lawyer, helping only himself, and some fatter cats, get rich" (168), and he places the pouch back in the drawer. That is, he recognizes the existence of what could be called an "identity crisis," but his first impulse is to reject the notion that his heritage might be of some avail. Sylvester's fanciful effort to envision his great-great grandfather on a raid is of a piece with his romanticized boyhood image of Lena Old Horn wearing buckskins and doing beadwork. The medicine pouch does resurface in the novel, but whether it acquires genuine symbolic force in the process, or serves as a sort of red herring, is debatable. At the end of the chapter, however, he does take it with him.

The eighth chapter records Sylvester's impulse or his instinctive urge to return to his Indian origins in one way or another, at least for confirmation of his plans to run for Congress. But his inclination toward his own Indianness remains curiously ambivalent, as he suppresses his desire to touch Lena, just as he did when he was in high school. The next chapter counters by portraying the sophisticated, urban world of Buster Harrington, the head of the law firm and a wheeler-dealer on the Montana political scene. The chapter ends with the announcement that Sylvester, who agrees to run for Congress, has been made a partner. Between these scenes the reader learns that Sylvester has not been seeing Shelley, but has wound up in bed three times with Patti Ann during the past week (187). When Harrington welcomes Sylvester to the congressional campaign, he emphasizes that his "activity will pay off" and that when he puts together his first piece of legislation, "[y]our people will reap the benefits" (193). Most important, he assures Yellow Calf that he will "make a difference," a phrase that may remind us of a paragraph early in the novel, in which he is described as "different" (38); the word is repeated three times in that paragraph.

In Chapter Ten the reader finds Shelley, sick with flu, becoming aware that her relationship with Sylvester Yellow Calf is disintegrating and at the same time recognizing that "deep down" she has gradually been made to feel "uncomfortable by his Indianness" when they are together in public (212). That is, Shelley's ambivalence parallels Sylvester's. In the latter half of the chapter the focus shifts to Patti Ann, who receives a phone call at work from a drunken ex-con named Woody Peters, whose blackmail threat compels her to confess to Sylvester her role in her husband's scheme. Sylvester perceives that Jack Harwood's blackmail plot is not only a way of getting himself out of prison, but also a way of "getting revenge" on the Indians who knifed him (225). Sylvester's initial anger over his betrayal quickly gives way to "sadness": both "the sadness of poverty" (227) and "the sadness of her loneliness" (228). But his plan of action is to put it all behind him until after the election. In short, although he correctly perceives that he has used Patti Ann as much as she has used him ("He had fucked her for his own selfish reasons" [228]), he remains as self-centered as ever. He does not appear to realize that such personal selfishness is likely to be at odds with a campaign platform that promises public selflessness.

In the next chapter Sylvester attempts to counter Woody Peters's blackmail scheme by having him sent back to prison, and he uses his connections to set him up. He associates his rather questionable ethics here with the jungle laws of the basketball court: "He had felt an anger and he recognized it from his basketball days, when he had gotten beaten badly by his man, a controlled anger and a resolve to make his man pay next time.

Sometimes he did it legally, sometimes illegally, sometimes brutally" (238). Sylvester realizes the plea bargaining by which Peters has wangled his release, despite a life of violent crime, is "all part of the game" (242), and he regards himself as one of the players. Sylvester plays the game dangerously when he dons a Cenex cap and drives Patti Ann's old Honda instead of his own flashy Saab to the Shanty bar to spy on Peters and his cohort Bobby Fitzgerald, and by the time he leaves, he is certain that Peters has recognized him. By this point in the novel, the plot has assumed the shape and dynamics of the novel of intrigue, and suspense builds in much the same way that it does in popular detective novels.[14] (The term "intrigue" is rarely employed in literary criticism except as it applies to drama and more specifically to "comedy of intrigue" or "situation," in which character is at least partially sacrificed for plot complexity. The most frequently cited example is William Congreve's *The Way of the World,* which appeared in 1700.)

In Chapter Twelve, Woody Peters sums up the thickening of the plot rather comically in his phone conversation with Jack Harwood: "Okay, so here's the situation. We know about him and your wife, he knows about Bobby and me and he knows about you and you know about him. It's all on the table, man. Everybody knows about everybody" (263). In another of Welch's artfully balanced and antithetical episodes, the reader first follows Jack's reflections on his seduction of Patti Ann, then moves to Woody's homoerotic relationship with Bobby. Like the other cons, Woody sees Harwood as "a mystery, a self-made loser" (277). Not surprisingly, the next twist of the plot is Woody's decision to double-cross Harwood, maybe "abuse"

Patti Ann in the process, then run off with Bobby to Mexico. Creating suspense for the reader, especially by arousing the reader's anxiety over sympathetic characters, is common to the novel of intrigue.

Just two days before Christmas (287), or perhaps three (290), as a delegation of Indians looks on, Sylvester announces for Congress on the steps of the administration building of a school in Helena for "unwanted children," where he has played Santa Claus on previous occasions. Although he feels uneasy about the "spectacle," which is a perfect cliché of such events, Yellow Calf consoles himself with the conviction that he will "make a difference," echoing in his thoughts the sentiment of Buster Harrington about a hundred pages earlier. In effect, Welch subtly suggests the transformation of Sylvester Yellow Calf from a man who was aware of his own difference even as a boy back on the reservation, to a man who is flattered into believing that he can "make a difference." As his political backers have implied from the outset, however, he will be forced to compromise his unique sense of himself as an individual in order to make that "difference." Sylvester's dilemma is that of any thoughtful person possessed of a social conscience: How to effect changes and reforms while remaining true to oneself. If he were a revolutionary, a potential Che Guevara attempting to force social change from the outside, that dilemma would not exist, because he would not need to concern himself with the maneuverings required to bring about change from within the system. But because he has committed himself to work legally and by conventional means, within the system, as a potential "insider," Sylvester's personal identity is vulnerable.

The scene verges on comedy when a boy from the school presents Yellow Calf with a plywood peace pipe, and he wonders what the cultural historian plans to do with it when he carries it away. When an Indian holy man blesses him with a smoking braid of sweet grass, Sylvester finds himself again consumed by ambivalence: "Caught up in the moment, Sylvester wished he had worn his greatgrandfather's war medicine. Then he thought that would be condescending, but he was now glad to have it in his possession. Just knowing that it was there made him feel aggressive and confident. Maybe the cultural historian had taken the peace pipe to put into some sort of archive" (293). Sylvester's mental leap from thinking of the medicine bag as the source of his confidence to supposing that the historian has placed the plywood peace pipe in a museum has various thematic implications. For example, one might conjecture that the Anglo culture is being doubly derided for the sterile symbolism of the plywood pipe and for regarding it as an historical artifact of some worth. Or one might suppose that, inasmuch as tribal elders are associated with the event, the Indians have lost touch with the genuine significance of the peace pipe, but on the other hand, one might argue that the presentation of a plywood pipe indicates the Indians' refusal to take such events as this one seriously. Whether Sylvester Yellow Calf places the proper value on the medicine bag also remains uncertain.

Shortly after Sylvester delivers his first speech, he comes home to find a blackmail note from Peters and Fitzgerald, and he realizes that Harwood is no longer in charge of the operation. But even as he becomes aware of his "sudden fall from grace" (303), Sylvester comes across a letter from the tribal council of the

Standing Rock Sioux in North Dakota, requesting that he do pro bono work for them on water rights issues, and the reader correctly surmises that this will be his way out of the tangled webs of intrigue. Peters and Fitzgerald's blackmail double-cross scheme quickly comes unraveled in Chapter Fourteen when Sylvester confronts them in Patti Ann's apartment and declares his intention of pulling out of the congressional race. In the next chapter he completes his "fall from grace" (327) as the new year approaches, telling Buster Harrington and Shelley everything that has happened over the past few months (since the middle of September, when Patti Ann first came to his office). Curiously, and without developing the idea, Welch introduces "an image of a dark bird," clearly drawn from *The Death of Jim Loney,* to haunt the law firm's New Year's Eve party (338). Yellow Calf spends the evening with Patti Ann, but "chastely." The decision not to remain lovers but to become friends confirms Sidner Larson's contention that by the end of the novel Sylvester proves his "ability to handle things without turning to the women in his life" (503–04).

In the last chapter, we learn that Sylvester's grandfather has died the following April and that Sylvester has been living in Bismarck and commuting to the Standing Rock reservation. He returns to Browning for the funeral, and in the final scene we see Lena Old Horn, as she leaves the area for good, watching Sylvester Yellow Calf shooting baskets by himself. She admires his "beauty and grace" and his "grace and intensity," both phrases that indicate the regeneration of his character (or soul) after the fall (349). Lena passes unnoticed as Sylvester plays his game in the wind and sleet, "going one on one against the only man who ever beat him" (349).

This final image, a sort of tableau vivant, is likely to linger in the minds of readers, and it suggests a variety of interpretations. The protagonist remains something of an outsider, both in the white world to which he had been apparently well assimilated and in the Indian worlds of both Montana and North Dakota (significantly, he does not live on the Sioux reservation, but drives in daily, often in harsh weather, from Bismarck, forty or fifty miles distant). On the other hand, he has overcome adversity and appears to be at ease with himself and the world, in a state of grace, at least implicitly, and triumphant over his adversaries. Yet he has failed, it seems, in his purpose, which was to "make a difference" in a fairly dramatic way that would touch upon the lives of the Indians and that would have broad economic, social, and ecological ramifications in the white world as well. But the door is clearly left open for a comeback of some sort; certainly, the final image does not suggest a man wallowing in defeat. Robert Gish celebrates Sylvester Yellow Calf as "a new warrior in a new West," but as Sidner Larson, Welch's Gros Ventre cousin, observes, "there is no easy resolution" in the novel.[15]

Gish sees Yellow Calf returning to the reservation "to reclaim the power of his great-great-grandfather" by incorporating "the old verities of loyalty to land and kin in the new Indian agenda," which "must include his assimilated 'whiteness,' as well as his rooted Indianness." The "New Warrior/New Ethnicity theme," Gish asserts, "is one of the most pervasive and convincing themes in the novel, one which in the Welch canon changes heretofore antiheroic characters into heroic ones and offers a counterpoint of future promise to past strains of elegy and apocalypse."[16] But Larson, himself a former businessman and lawyer in Montana and now a professor at the University of Oregon, argues that "[t]hings are more complicated than they seem, especially with regard to the emergence of the middle-class Indian."[17] Larson sees no evidence "that Yellow Calf has overcome his feelings of inadequacy" by the end of the novel, "and many would say he has not progressed by electing to work on Indian water rights."[18] As Larson observes, Sylvester has not found a "home" in either Browning or Helena, but, like Lena Old Horn, has gone away in order to start over. In the process, Welch seems to depart from the prevalent "homing" plot detected by William Bevis in other Native American novels, despite the fact that in the last scene Sylvester Yellow Calf is back in Browning.[19] Not surprisingly, Bevis regards Sylvester's final choice as "perhaps the darkest aspect of the book," which he believes "seems to suggest a kind of salvation through renouncing power."[20]

The Indian Lawyer combines elements of the novel of character with those of the historical novel in such a way that psychology mingles with sociology at the turn of nearly every page. The novel reflects James Welch's ongoing fascination with problems of identity, particularly as such problems have an ethnic aspect, but arguably, more than in any of the previous novels, the issue of character turns on an ethical rather than an ethnic axis. The recurrent medicine bag, with its connections to similar objects in both *Winter in the Blood* and *Fools Crow,* remains something of a red herring in this novel. Sylvester picks it up, but he does not carry it with him. Its value to him in whatever political or sexual combat he encounters is slight, for its mythology is not alive for him, despite his awareness of its historical and familial significance. While his grandmother tends to honor the old traditions, his grandfather is "a rational man" who does not "believe in that hocus-pocus," either tribal or Christian (344). In many ways, the dilemma of the Native American today is that of the speaker in Matthew Arnold's "Stanzas from the Grand Chartreuse": "Wandering between two worlds, one dead, / The other powerless to be born." Perhaps the most positive element of Indianness in the novel is its intertribalism. To a far greater degree than Welch's other protagonists, Sylvester is aware of the common cause among all Indians. Lena Old Horn is Crow, traditional enemy of the Blackfeet, yet she works for years on the Blackfeet reservation. While at Stanford, Sylvester had a romantic relationship with a Laguna woman; late in the novel he becomes interested in Navajo problems; and at the end, he is working for the Sioux. Whether this constitutes a meaningful step toward what Elizabeth Cook-Lynn refers to as "First Nation ideology," may be debatable, but clearly Sylvester Yellow Calf, who starts out as a type of the egocentric character she appears to condemn, ends up with a radically altered sense of who he is and of the kind of difference he can make in the world.[21]

Unlike any of the earlier novels, however, *The Indian Lawyer* reaches into what some readers may consider to be forbidden territory, the land of popular fiction. While fellow writer Rick DeMarinis describes the novel as "an unforgettable morality play" in his dust jacket blurb, the editors note on the inside flap that it exhibits "the tension of the psychological thriller." While Gary Davenport praised the novel for its "thematic use of Montana locations," he objected that its characters "operate mainly on the level of the 'serious' dramatic television series: that is to say, their minds, their problems, and the intellectual vantage

from which they are observed are to a large degree standard-
ized."[22] Not enough time has elapsed since its publication for a
full and valid assessment of the critical response to *The Indian
Lawyer,* but in adapting the techniques of the novel of intrigue
(from clearly defined villains, like Harwood and Peters, to plot
twists like the motif of the con being conned by other cons)
Welch has taken the sort of risk that most novelists whose works
are regarded as "literary" take from time to time. Presumably, the
complexity of Sylvester Yellow Calf as a character and the significance of the issues he confronts, along with Welch's refusal
to offer an easy, pat conclusion will prove sufficient to cause the
novel to be taken seriously.

CHAPTER SEVEN

Custer as Native American Text

James Welch's only foray into nonfiction to date is the provocatively titled *Killing Custer* (1994), a title that might call to mind Peter Matthiessen's powerful historical novel, *Killing Mister Watson,* which was published in 1990. (Welch comments on Matthiessen's *Crazy Horse* in an interview conducted in the spring of 1995.)[1] At the prompting of his editor, Jerry Howard, Welch began writing the book in December of 1991, after working with filmmaker Paul Stekler on the documentary filmscript for *Last Stand at Little Bighorn,* which debuted on 25 November 1992, "the day before Thanksgiving," on PBS and "turned out to be a great success."[2] Thanksgiving is a holiday that Indians tend to greet with mixed emotions. The mixed-blood Jim Loney has only vague memories of Thanksgiving, although he does recall boyhood celebrations of Christmas and Easter. In the novel, the holiday is presented as a sort of antitype of the image familiar from Norman Rockwell's covers for the old *Saturday Evening Post:* "Thanksgiving and the streets were empty. Loney walked slowly, eating a piece of bread and trying to think what it had been like with his aunt."[3] In *The Indian Lawyer* Sylvester's world is beginning to fall apart by the time Thanksgiving arrives, but the holiday means little to him: "Thanksgiving had come and gone and Sylvester had missed it. . . . He had been a little uncomfortable about celebrating Thanksgiving anyway—it wasn't really a festive occasion for Indians."[4]

Although Welch shares the credit for this book with Stekler, noting in his acknowledgments that "it wouldn't have occurred to me to write such a book" without his "inspiration" (9), Stekler's direct contribution appears to be limited to a ten-page afterword. Poets have become novelists over the years, and both poets and novelists have turned to nonfiction from time to time, but they usually turn to such varieties of the genre as memoir, and more recently to the current rage, "creative nonfiction." *Killing Custer,* however, as the subtitle implies (*The Battle of the Little Bighorn and the Fate of the Plains Indians*), is a historical text; moreover, Welch was keenly aware in undertaking the project that he was exploring what "may be the most depicted event in our nation's history," about which "hundreds of books" have been written, "thousands of illustrations" made, and "at least forty films" produced (22). Consequently, the question, as Welch phrases it, was, "What can one say about the battle that hasn't been said before?" (21) He responds that new studies, some of which concern artifacts uncovered in a 1983 range fire, have brought fresh evidence to light, and that information supplied by Indians who participated in the battle is now being given greater credit than in the past. After all, as Welch points out, contrary to popular opinion, there *were* survivors of the "massacre"; they just happened to be Sioux and Cheyenne (22).

Killing Custer is really two books, one dealing with the battle, and more important its aftermath, from an Indian perspective, which was Stekler's intention with the film, and the other concerning the experience of making the film. Welch does not claim to be a professional historian, and as he states from the outset, it does not "provide any startling revelations from a historical or military standpoint" (22). Rather, he suggests, the book is intended to "offer the reader a comprehensive frontier environment which will provide an explanation for why this battle had to take place" (22) and to aid readers in their understanding of "this nation's treatment of the first Americans" (23). In addition to a couple of maps and a chronology, Welch and Stekler provide seventy illustrations, ranging from a nineteenth-century ledger drawing of Custer's cavalry column under attack at Little Bighorn by Red Horse, a Miniconjou Dakota, to a group photo of Welch with the production crew of the film. Historians have not responded to the book with great eagerness. Neil C. Mangum expresses disappointment in the fact that only one chapter directly concerns the battle, points out several "problems of fact," and argues that Indian interpretations of the battle *have* received adequate attention.[5] Richard White complains that "he treats the intricacies of history with a heavy-handedness that would make him wince if this were fiction."[6] David Cremean finds the book "uneven" and suggests that "Welch never seems entirely at home in the nonfictional world."[7]

On the other hand, the book won Welch the Western Literature Association's Distinguished Achievement Award for 1994, and Cremean, noting that "the book is best when personal," concludes that it is "worthwhile, engaging reading."[8] Richard White appropriately characterizes it as "less a straightforward history than an intelligent and thoughtful man's meditation on a particular historical event,"[9] and writing for the *New Statesman,* Helen Carr describes the book as "evocatively and compellingly written."[10] In an interview, parts of which have not been published, Welch describes the book as "a little autobiography, a lot of pure historical narrative, and some short moments of personal observation," he declares himself "happy with it," partly because it is so "multifaceted."[11] Welch sees the story of "Custer's Last Stand" as the American version of a "kind of worldwide myth," the "idea of being overrun by hordes of savages, a different race. Part of the white myth is that a small, well-armed, well-disciplined group of whites with high moral values can't lose to a bunch of savages, and I think it's that arrogance that white cultures have brought with them all over the world into native lands. . . . People want to know how a group of white men could have been wiped out like that. It's almost like everyone's worst nightmare."[12]

Welch's first chapter focuses on the massacre of 173 Blackfeet, mostly women and children, on the Marias River, which occurred six years before the battle on the Little Bighorn in June of 1876 and which was the culminating event of *Fools Crow*. As Welch observes, this catastrophe was "more representative of what happened to Indian people who resisted the white invasion than Custer's Last Stand" (23); moreover, the event is part of his own heritage, his great grandmother, Red Paint Woman, having been a member of Heavy Runner's unfortunate band. What gives this chapter its appeal, however, is not so much the historical observations, some of which are drawn from John C. Ewers's *The Blackfeet: Raiders on the Northwestern Plains,* which was an important source of *Fools Crow,* but his personal quest for the exact site of the massacre, where Heavy Runner's peaceful band was attacked even as he frantically waved his copy of a treaty. Historical figures like the trader, Malcolm Clark, and the renegade warrior, Owl Child, will be familiar to those who have read Welch's novel, but the characters who participate directly in the drama of discovery are Welch's wife Lois and friend Bill Bevis.

The element of personal narrative calls for descriptive writing of the sort that reminds the reader that Welch began his career as a poet: "What we had come to see lay just below the promontory—the Big Bend of the Marias [pronounced "mar-AI-as"]. And the landscape was black. The valley floor, the cliffs and ridges above it, the scrub brush upon it, even the river—all black beneath the gray sky. The only flashes of light were the windward sides of silvery sagebrush bending beneath the relentless north wind" (42–43). The images are vivid, the sound patterns are musical (note the alliterative "s" and "b" sounds near the end along with the assonance that links "bending," "relentless," and "wind"), and the rhythm could be scanned by anyone with a feeling for meter. But the burden of this chapter has to do with questions: "Why, then, is Custer's Last Stand such an important part of this nation's history, and why is the Massacre on the Marias known to so few people?" (44). And later, "Was Custer a fool who rode to his death, as Sitting Bull, the great Sioux leader, stated, or was he a martyr who died in the cause of righteousness, as both the frontier and eastern press contended?" (46). Welch concludes that it does not matter much that some considered Custer a fool and others a hero; what matters is that he died, and his death "was proof that the Indians were savages and should be dealt with just as the whites dealt with all the savages they encountered around the world" (46).

Killing Custer is Welch's most outspokenly political book to date, and he ends the first chapter as follows: "Custer's Last Stand has gone down in history as an example of what savagery the Indians were capable of; the Massacre on the Marias is a better example of what man is capable of doing to man"(47). In his interview with Dennis Held, Welch says, "I got most of my rage out" in writing *Fools Crow*,[13] but Chapter One of *Killing Custer* might suggest to some readers that they are about to embark on an angry book, perhaps a predictable diatribe or an indictment of sorts. This does not prove to be the case, however, for as Welch responded to the question whether he felt pressured to "rewrite history" with the film (and the book that followed), "we didn't make the Indians all good guys and the whites all bad guys."[14]

In his 1995 interview with Welch, William Bevis applauded "the fact that *Killing Custer* was actually about killing Sitting Bull" and that in the process, Welch had "subverted the entire project."[15] By the end of the second chapter, which opens with an account of the sacred Sun Dance ceremony, particularly the details of the one held in June of 1876, when Sitting Bull announced his vision of the coming defeat of the bluecoats, it is apparent that the Sioux chief will be at least as important to the book as the white lieutenant colonel. Welch reflects on Custer's record during the Civil War, but he focuses more intently on Custer's reputation as a harsh disciplinarian, one result of which was his conviction in a court-martial held in 1867. After a year of suspension from command without pay, Custer was back in the West, at General Phil Sheridan's request, in the winter of 1868, when he struck the Cheyenne village of Black Kettle on the Washita. Welch's report of the casualties is representative of his effort to remain neutral on such controversial matters: "The firing ceased and 103 Cheyennes lay dead in the snow and mud. Custer reported that they were fighting men, but others said that ninety-two of them were women, children, and old people" (62). Welch then highlights the killing of Black Kettle and his wife, not only pointing out that the elderly couple (Black Kettle was sixty-seven) were shot in the back, but also by closing the paragraph with a vivid portrait of the discovering of their bodies, "trampled and covered with mud" (62). Even supposedly un- aligned academic historians are rarely able to be as objective as they intend to be, and of course Welch makes no such claims for himself as a commentator. As to the Black Hills treaty signed by Red Cloud, Welch notes, "It is clear that neither side intended to honor the agreement" (69).

Although Chapter Three concerns primarily the stock mar- ket crash and resultant depression that followed in the Panic of 1873, which brought extra pressure on the gold-rich Black Hills shortly after the treaty was signed in 1875, some readers will be more attracted to the pages in which Welch recounts his first visit to the Little Bighorn battlefield in 1974 and reflects on injustices against Indians that were brought to light by the American Indian Movement (AIM) and its leaders, Dennis Banks and Russell Means. Welch's comments on recent historical events take up relatively little of Chapter Three, but they dominate the fourth chapter, which begins with his memories of his first visit, when he and his Anglo wife were harassed by a park ranger for eating lunch in the back of their Volkswagen bus because "this is a national monument" and "you're not allowed to eat here" (96). Welch's response seems appropriate, given the circumstances: "We thanked him for pointing out our sacrilege, and when he turned away to attend to other duties I gave him the finger. I was young then" (96).[16] Welch also reflects on movie treatments of the

Plains Indians, praising *Little Big Man* for "the feat of humanizing Indians" (98), but expressing reservations about *Dances with Wolves.* He also records the change of designation from "Custer Battlefield National Monument" to "Little Bighorn Battlefield National Monument" in 1991, but as he observes, it is not evident that much of the profits from the tourist attraction appear to have found their way into the coffers of the Crow, who served as Custer's scouts and on whose reservation the site is located: "A very large motel complex, built not too many years ago by the Crow tribe, sprawls on the edge of Interstate 90, vandalized, and falling down" (102). He also comments on the three years that Barbara Booher, of Cherokee-Ute descent, spent as superintendent of the battlefield: "She was the perfect person for the job" (107).

What makes the book engaging, however, is not so much the blending of contemporary and historical reflections on the battle and on the battlefield as it is Welch's creation of scenarios. At the end of the chapter, Welch imagines the "hubbub" in the Indian camp as the soldiers approached: "But you are sitting on the bank of a slightly off-color river and what you really hear is magpies and an occasional meadowlark, or a cow calling her calf to remind you that you are here, now, nearly in the twenty-first century" (110). Such moments recall Welch's comments to interviewers about how he undertook the writing of his first novel, *Winter in the Blood:* "When I first started thinking about a piece of prose writing, I thought it was going to be a travel piece."[17]

Chapter Five concerns Crazy Horse, and particularly his defeat of a large force under General Crook on the Rosebud just eight days before the Battle of the Little Bighorn. Had Custer known of that battle, Welch observes, he might have reconnoitered the huge village properly: "But his impatience with proper reconnaissance, borne of a constant fear that the Indians would escape him, eventually would lead to disaster" (127). Custer also opted to decline the use of Gatling guns because they were "too cumbersome," and, more important, he turned down the offer of four companies from the Second Cavalry. But just as Welch depicts Custer on the verge of the attack at the end of the fifth chapter, he surprises the reader and creates suspense by devoting the next chapter to commentary on the Plains Indians, their use of horses, their buffalo hunting, and their "love of pageantry" (140). This culminates in several pages of commentary on the "problematic" matter of torture and mutilation by the Plains Indians (141), but Welch has little difficulty exculpating them in light of European practices extending from Achilles dragging the body of Hector behind his chariot, to Colonel John Chivington's massacre and dismemberment of Cheyennes at Sand Creek in 1864, and on again to the atrocities of World War II and Vietnam. As Welch suggests, the "thunderous applause" accorded to the hundred Indian scalps that Chivington displayed on the stage of a theater in Denver (144) has no metaphysical basis to compare with the "purpose" that made sense to the Indians: "It was clear to the Indians that their enemies would be there in the world behind this one, the real world, and an enemy without arms or legs or a head could do them no harm there" (147).

Predictably, Welch saves his lengthiest chapter (it is nearly twice as long as the others) for the battle, and perhaps it is no coincidence that it is the seventh (Custer's unit having been the Seventh Cavalry) or that it begins almost exactly at the center of the text. Welch reflects on the heat of that day (nearly a hundred

degrees), and he speculates on why the Indians were not better prepared for the attack, despite warnings the day before from a
Cheyenne prophet named Box Elder (154). He castigates Major
Reno as "faint-hearted" (155), and he reflects on Sitting Bull's
absence during the fight (at forty-two, he suggests, the Sioux chief
was too old for combat; moreover, he had undergone considerable
suffering in the Sun Dance ceremony). In response to frequently
posed questions, like why did Custer divide his forces in the face
of a superior enemy, Welch sensibly refers to authorities like
John S. Gray, whose book *Custer's Last Campaign* (1991) he cites
fairly often. Throughout his account of the battle, Welch focuses
on the reports of Indians who participated, from Custer's Crow
scout, Curley, to warriors like Gall and Wooden Leg and including Indians like Kate Bighead who witnessed parts of the action.

Welch debunks a number of popular myths and legends that
have grown up around the battle, including the notion that a
Cheyenne woman named Me-o-tzi (also known as Mo-nah-se-
tah, a name that might be familiar to those who have read Norman Maclean's *A River Runs through It and Other Stories*) was
the mother of a child by Custer (173) and the story that Custer's
body was left unmutilated and his scalp left intact out of respect.
Of the latter myth, Welch notes that Custer was prematurely
bald, "and what hair he had left was cut short. Long Hair's scalp
was not worth taking" (177). Welch does not avoid unpleasant
facts, however, noting that the story of Rain-in-the-Face's boast
that he would eat the heart of the colonel's brother Tom because
he had arrested and jailed him two years earlier appears proba-
ble: "At the Little Bighorn, Tom Custer's heart was missing. He
lay facedown, arrows bristling in his back, his entrails leaking

out of him, all his scalp removed, the back of his head so smashed it looked flat" (177). That is, Welch does not avoid the gruesome details of the mutilations that followed the battle, including the beheading of Bloody Knife, Custer's favorite Arikara-Hunkpapa Sioux scout (181). As Welch notes, the disaster "completely ruined the centennial celebration" in Philadelphia with its exhibits of the nation's industrial might (189). But the Indians retreated in the face of the large body of reinforcements that arrived too late, and the great massing of tribes was not to occur again: "At this point, they had no more illusions of life as it used to be, of following the buffalo herds forever, of freedom. They only wanted one last summer before they were killed or put on the reservation" (195–96).

In Chapter Eight, which may be the best in the book, Welch records his return to the battlefield in the fall of 1990 with Paul Stekler and others to work on the film for PBS. Welch meanders casually between historically charged events of the past and sometimes random encounters in the present that, in a way, have also become "historical." For example, in the "funky" (202) hotel at Lodge Grass (population about 800), located twenty miles south of the battlefield, he runs into an eighty-five-year-old black cowboy named Bill: "His laugh was deep, but nervous, as though he had spent many years getting out of people's way" (203). After providing a quick character sketch of Bill, Welch reflects on the death of Isaiah Dorman, "the only black man on the Custer expedition" (204), and he wonders how he was treated by the other soldiers and officers. Noting that Dorman had married a Sioux woman and served as a translator, Welch adds that "a surprising number of black men have been welcomed into western tribes, marrying Indian women, fathering children," but he is quick to observe that this spirit of tolerance is not universal: Some Indians "are downright racist toward other people as oppressed as themselves. A sad fact" (204).

Welch then recounts their first interview, a "complete disaster" (204) resulting from the tribal elder's greed. The dilemma is made all the more uncomfortable as the elder, who has "a touch of the confidence man in him" (206), is quick to point out how past Indian informants have been exploited by anthropologists, historians, and moviemakers, a charge that Welch recognizes as often valid. In the end, however, Welch concludes that "the old man had ceased to be an elder and had become simply an old man bickering over money" (208). Despite their recognition that he would have "sounded great on film," they decide they cannot afford him (208). Against this unnamed elder, Welch balances three more cooperative Indians who prove to be very important to the project: Bill Tall Bull, tribal historian of the Northern Cheyenne; Ted Rising Sun, a Cheyenne in his seventies who served in both World War II and Korea and who was "the most decorated Indian in the Korean War" (209); and Joe Medicine Crow, nearly eighty, and the grandson of one of Custer's Crow scouts. Also a tribal historian, Medicine Crow received a master's degree from the University of Southern California in 1939 and was starting work on a doctorate when the war intervened; this, in "a time when it was rare for an Indian to go to college, much less graduate school" (213).

As he moves through the chapter, Welch weaves reflections on the battle and its aftermath; for example, on the hasty burial of the bodies and on a letter concerning a business deal that indicates Custer's need for money, drawn from the archives by museum curator Kitty Deernose, a Crow Indian. Like many of their "favorite toys" (218), that letter had to be left out of the film script, which in its final form was to run only twenty-two pages. Also left out of the film, but recounted in the book, is the tragic journey in 1866 of Bill Thomas, who kept a diary, his son Charley, and a mule driver named Joe Schultz. Welch and Paul Stekler track down Bill Thomas's grave site near Interstate 90, and of the artifacts, including the diary, he writes, "In these items we saw hope, misunderstanding, conflict—and finally, nothing more than a moment in history that does whiz by like cars on the interstate" (221).

The Thomas episode is indicative of Welch's compassion for all sides involved in the darker aspects of the history of the American West. Interestingly, he concludes the chapter with an account of a run-in with a "mystery guest," who turns out to be the most prominent American Indian Movement leader, Russell Means. His appearance at the Elks Club outside Hardin is at least as uncomfortable for those involved in the film project, including Superintendent Booher, as the earlier meeting with the uncooperative tribal elder. Means at first appears "hostile and abrupt," and Welch notes how well Booher "negotiates" the "tricky terrain" (225). With the coming of dinner, Means becomes more sociable, less the activist than the "raconteur": "He was Russell Means and he could not forget that, but he gave his image a rest for this one night" (226). Welch's decision to recount this episode, and particularly to conclude one of his strongest chapters with it, exemplifies his stance on Native American political issues. Not an activist by nature, Welch is, however, on the record as approving much of what has been achieved through the efforts and energies of AIM and Red Power movements: "I think that activist Indian pride did have a positive effect on young people and on succeeding generations. That was 20 to 25 years ago. I think the idea that they were radical, that they went overboard in a sense, is just what Indian people needed at that time. They needed Indians, like Blacks, to just get in there and really raise hell."[18] On the other hand, when Barbara Booher called him a week after their dinner at the Elks Club and told him that Means was interested in having him write his biography, Welch did not return the call.

In the ninth chapter Welch recounts the aftermath of the Battle of the Little Bighorn, the pursuit of Sitting Bull into Canada, where he stayed until 1881, and the surrender and eventual pursuit of Crazy Horse, after he left the reservation, by a force ironically twice as large as Custer's famous command. The chapter ends with the killing of Crazy Horse by soldiers when he resisted being placed in prison. With Chapter Ten, which returns to the story of Sitting Bull, Welch completes what William Bevis has argued is a "subversion" of his supposed project, which readers might assume would be to tell all about Custer. As Welch, agreeing with Bevis, puts it, "Custer was as subservient a character as I could possibly make him and still be in the picture."[19] By the time of his surrender in July of 1881, just five years after the Battle of the Little Bighorn, Sitting Bull's forces, that had once numbered in the thousands, with some 1,500 warriors, had dwindled to 187. The killing of Custer is diminished in almost every way by Welch's account of the killing of Sitting Bull, who appears ragged and demoralized at the time of his surrender and is bewildered at his status as a "celebrity" (258). Struggling to maintain his authority, the fifty-three-year-old chief in 1884 succeeds fairly well on the reservation as a farmer, and he spends several months in 1885 with Buffalo Bill's Wild West show, but the Dawes Severalty Act of 1887 and subsequent legislation pares away at the reservations, and when Wovoka leads the Plains Indians in the Ghost Dance movement of 1890, Sitting Bull is forced to go along, even though, Welch observes, he was "definitely skeptical" of the new religion (268). At the last, it is a force of forty-four Indian policemen who pull the chief from his bed and, in the melee that follows, shoot him down. Two weeks later, Welch notes, on 29 December 1890, "Custer's old outfit," the Seventh Cavalry, put a bloody end to the last Indian uprising in the West at Wounded Knee (271).

In his epilogue Welch retells a few events that occurred during the filming of *Last Stand at Little Bighorn,* the most vivid of which takes place on Reno Hill during a storm as he watches the distant fires set in the vicinity of the Indian encampment: "Perhaps it was the fire, the thunder, lightning, and rain, but I imagined I could hear the voices of mourning women carried by the wind. I thought if I walked up to the upper bench where the large village really stood I would see a small group of Lakotas and Cheyennes standing silently, watching the fires, watching us, thinking of long-ago fires. Perhaps they would know that their ancestors were safe in the real world behind this one" (278). Welch then quickly summarizes the rapid evolution of the Custer myth, pushed by the press and most vigorously promoted by Buffalo Bill Cody and the colonel's young widow, Libbie. Welch expresses surprise that Lakota and Cheyenne people with whom he talked do not consider the Battle of the Little Bighorn to be "the major event in their tribal memory" (285). The events they commemorate are not the greatest of their victories, but rather such tragedies as the killing of Crazy Horse and Sitting Bull or the massacre at Wounded Knee. Loss, Welch concludes, "stays with a people" (285).

Asked by Dennis Held what he hoped his film and book would accomplish, James Welch replied, "I think the film did what my hopes were—it reached a large audience, millions of people, and people seemed to think it was done honestly and fairly. And if that's the picture they get—a fair, honest picture of the Battle of the Little Bighorn and the events that led up to it—they'll be educated, and I think they'll be more sympathetic to the Indians of that period. They weren't noble savages, they weren't bloodthirsty savages, they were people with families, they had a very well-developed society. And I hope people come away with that understanding, because our ignorance certainly contributes to the tragedy of what happened to the Indians of that period."[20] Implicit in Welch's statement, perhaps, is the subtext of *Killing Custer,* which is that "our ignorance" also contributes to the tragedy of what is happening to many Indians right now.

In an essay published in 1988 Dexter Westrum described *Fools Crow* as "fat, rambling, and almost loud, although no less finely done" than James Welch's first two novels. He also observed that Welch had developed a large cast of characters and was "working, for the first time, with subplots."[1] Although *Winter in the Blood* may remain Welch's most popular novel with most readers, *Fools Crow* is likely to be regarded increasingly as his pivotal work. Westrum sees the title character as "the spiritual archetype of the contemporary Welch protagonists" and adds that "in the character of Fools Crow we see the life force that drives his contemporary counterparts onward."[2] Westrum made these observations at least two years before *The Indian Lawyer* was published, but Fools Crow appears to be as much the "spiritual archetype" for Sylvester Yellow Calf as he is for Jim Loney and the unnamed narrator of *Winter in the Blood.* What defines Fools Crow as a character—courage, compassion, integrity, and wisdom—a firm, but not complacent, sense of who he is and of his place in the world—is what Welch's other protagonists lack and desire. But is that possible for them?

Westrum argues that it is Fools Crow's "tribal identity" that accounts for his self-knowledge and self-confidence, and he concludes that "Welch's protagonists discover purpose when they discover who they are."[3] The great dilemma of Welch's main characters other than Fools Crow is how to establish self-identity and a concomitant sense of purpose without the support of the tribe, but with what one might describe as a vestigial, haunting memory (one is tempted to say, after Jung, a "collective unconscious") of the tribe. In effect, then, the prevailing theme in Welch's writing concerns the familiar, modern, existential identity crisis: What am I if all a priori definitions of what I am are regarded as null and void? Only Fools Crow is free, to a large extent at any rate and free in a purposive (nonabsurd) universe, of the crushing responsibility of defining himself in a world in which, implicitly, "existence precedes essence." In such a world all self-definitions are necessarily subjective to the point of solipsism, and all identities are in a constant, nervous state of flux or of "becoming," rather than in a steady, calm state of composure or of "being."

To the extent that traditional tribal value systems provided a priori definition of the self for Native Americans and other tribal peoples of the world, the community, with its traditional religious value systems, provided such definition for Americans, Europeans, and other nontribal peoples of the world. The implied premise here is that of the past tense; that is the vulnerable first premise of the loose syllogism—given that such systems are defunct. Of course, while many non-Indians are likely to concede readily that the system of traditional tribal values is defunct, they may not be quite so agreeable to the premise that the system of traditional religious values as embodied in the Eurocentric idea of community is defunct. Nevertheless, the point is important, if not vital, to assessing the impact of Welch's novels outside the rather constricted community of Native American readers and scholars. If non-Indian readers simply regard Welch's novels as social commentaries on a certain section of the population that can be described as "them" or "not us," then the universal appeal of his writing is severely constrained, and Welch's early fear of being regarded as merely "a good Indian writer" instead of "a good writer" will be substantiated.

An important corollary to the premise asserted above is that the current surge of religious fundamentalism, which appears to be reflected in the recent enthusiasm in the United States for homeschooling and charter schools and is therefore not simply limited to matters of theology, is not a sign that traditional values are still viable, but a sign that without the sustenance of tribe or community, people become fearful to the point of desperation. Recent events as different in nature, apparently, as the Branch Davidian cult that ended disastrously in Waco, Texas, and the Taliban takeover in Afghanistan, a victory for the most reactionary version of Islam, reflect the extremes to which frightened people will go in order to reestablish what they would most likely insist are "traditional values" of the tribe or community.

Typically, with the notable exception of Fools Crow, Welch strips his protagonists not only of tribe and community (Sylvester Yellow Calf's connection with the community or with what critical theorists might term "the culture of the dominant ideology" is tenuous at best), but also of family, at least in any consistent or coherent sense. Despite his education and prosperity, Sylvester is not much better off in these respects than the narrator of *Winter in the Blood.* All of his protagonists, again with the exception of Fools Crow, should strike us with a feeling of uneasiness. Not one of them can hold onto or establish love or beauty in his life, and although it could be argued that each of them arrives at some sort of justice, it happens that justice, even in some Platonic form that does not involve retribution, provides rather cold comfort at the end of the day. All of his protagonists, including Fools Crow, so far as the reader can infer his destiny, are victims. Only Jim Loney is taken to the extreme, but if Welch remains skeptical as to the human potential for significant change, as he indicated in interviews about *Winter in the Blood,* it may well be that *The Death of Jim Loney* offers the only ending that can be described as "satisfying," an ending wherein the protagonist's life becomes a completed work of art.

Of course to say that *The Death of Jim Loney* provides a certain, almost paradoxical sense of "satisfaction" for the reader, is not to say it is Welch's best novel. Every writer hopes, and must to some extent believe, that his or her best novel is the next one, the one he or she is writing now. In Welch's case that novel is *The Heartsong of Charging Elk,* which, from the author's synopsis, promises to sustain most of the features that have characterized his fiction to date. The subject, again, is Indians. The dominant theme, again, will concern the protagonist's efforts to define himself. But perhaps the most important feature of Welch's fiction, as this study has attempted to demonstrate, has been its remarkable variety, particularly as it has been shown by the *kinds,* or subgenres, of novel he writes. In *The Heartsong of Charging Elk* Welch will locate his protagonist outside of Montana, a move for which he prepared his readers, to some extent, by breaking the "homing" pattern at the end of *The Indian Lawyer,* which finds Sylvester Yellow Calf living in Bismarck, North Dakota, and working with the Sioux.

The Heartsong of Charging Elk will be an international novel, and it might very well prompt some comparisons with the novels of Henry James. "This novel," Welch writes, "is the story of a young Oglala (Sioux) man who goes to France at the age of 25 with Buffalo Bill's Wild West show in 1889 and never returns to his home in the Dakotas."[4] While *The Heartsong of Charging Elk* will be a historical novel of sorts, like *Fools Crow,* it will be very much unlike that novel in most other ways. Charging Elk, the protagonist, is illiterate, and for the first several years he speaks neither English nor French. Some readers will readily connect the general outlines of the novel with events from *Black Elk Speaks* (1932, 1961), at least up to a point. At age twenty-three, in the summer of 1886, Black Elk, also an Oglala Sioux, joined Buffalo Bill's Wild West show and toured Europe for about three years, during which time he fell ill, as does Charging Elk, and was cared for by a "Wasichu [white] girl" in Paris.[5] Black Elk, however, returned to his people, while Charging Elk never does.

One feature that will distinguish *The Heartsong of Charging Elk* from Welch's other novels to date is that it covers a fairly broad expanse of time (sixteen years, from 1889 to 1905). By the time the Wild West show returns to France in 1905, Charging Elk has gone through a considerable ordeal, which includes homicide, a sensational trial, prison, and marriage to a young French woman. From the synopsis it is apparent that the plot will be far more involved than has been the case with Welch's other novels. When Charging Elk talks with the young Oglala men who are members of the show, he sees that he must make a choice between staying in France and returning to his home, but he recognizes that things have changed considerably in the aftermath of the Ghost Dance and the massacre at Wounded Knee in 1890, and he elects to stay in France. As Welch succinctly sums up the ending in his synopsis, "The novel ends with the birth of a son. His decision was a good one."

Welch writes, "This novel is about a person who has spent his entire life either outside of society or living on the fringes." As a boy, Welch notes, Charging Elk lived off the reservation and followed the old ways, as did Black Elk, and in France he is "a complete outsider" because he is illiterate and at first understands neither English nor French. Welch, who has made two trips to France in the process of researching the context for this novel, describes the attitude of the French toward Indians at the turn of the century as "ambivalent—on the one hand, they considered the Indian a noble savage, a member of a vanishing race; on the other hand, they considered him a savage, perhaps not even human." This novel, which will tell of Charging Elk's struggle with these conflicting attitudes toward his identity, will likely generate a good deal of controversy, particularly if readers obsessed with the issue of "Indianness" in Welch's novels are offended by the implications of the concluding phrase of his synopsis, which indicates that the protagonist "eventually becomes a Frenchman."

Whether assimilation is a dream or a nightmare, and whether or not it is even genuinely possible, remains a volatile issue for Native Americans and for students and scholars involved in the growing field (or discipline) of Native American studies. Throughout his writing, James Welch has investigated the intricacies of personal identity: what it is to be human, what it is to be a man, what it is to be Indian, what it is to be of mixed blood, what it is to be isolated and confused, what it is to be a leader and self-confident. Sylvester Yellow Calf comes very close to achieving insider status in *The Indian Lawyer,* but as Sidner Larson observes, he is not only rejected by the white society to which he very nearly gains not only access, but power and influence, but he also becomes "an outsider to family, landscape, and tribal identity."[6] The implications of Welch's synopsis of his forthcoming novel are that it is possible, and presumably desirable, for an outsider to become an insider. The synopsis also appears to suggest that an individual may successfully create, or re-create, his or her identity, that an individual may fabricate an altogether different self. But at what price, some readers will surely ask.

Chapter One: "My Subject Has Been Indians"

1. Nicholas O'Connell, *At the Field's End: Interviews with 20 Pacific Northwest Writers* (Seattle: Madrona, 1987) 62.

2. Ibid., 62, 65.

3. Ron McFarland and M. K. Browning, "An Interview with James Welch," *James Welch,* ed. Ron McFarland (Lewiston, ID: Confluence, 1986) 13.

4. Charles R. Larson, *American Indian Fiction* (Albuquerque: U of New Mexico P, 1978) 140. See also Reynolds Price's review of the novel in the *New York Times Book Review* 10 Nov. 1974: 1.

5. Charles R. Larson, review of *Winter in the Blood, New Republic* 14 Dec. 1974: 26; Roger Sale, review of *Winter in the Blood, New York Review of Books* 12 Dec. 1974: 20.

6. Alan R. Velie, *Four American Indian Literary Masters* (Norman: U of Oklahoma P, 1982) 92.

7. Kathleen Sands, "*The Death of Jim Loney:* Indian or Not?" *Studies in American Indian Literature* (Fall 1981): 8; reprinted in *James Welch,* ed. McFarland 132.

8. Peter Wild, *James Welch,* Western Writers Series 57 (Boise, ID: Boise State UP, 1983) 45.

9. William W. Bevis, "James Welch," *Updating the Literary West* (Fort Worth: Texas Christian UP, 1997) 813.

10. O'Connell 67.

11. Wild 17.

12. McFarland and Browning 4.

13. Robert Gish, "The Word Medicine of James Welch," *Beyond Bounds: Cross-Cultural Essays on Anglo, American Indian, and Chicano Literature* (Albuquerque: U of New Mexico P, 1996) 70.

14. Bevis, "James Welch" 820.

15. Louis Owens, "'From the Inside Out': Identity and Authenticity in James Welch's *Fools Crow,*" *Cresset* 55 (Nov. 1991): 9.

16. Edward Hoagland, review of *Indian Lawyer, New York Times Book Review* 25 Nov. 1990: 7; William Hoagland, review of *Indian Lawyer, Western American Literature* 26 (Fall 1991): 256.

17. Lee Lemon, review of *Indian Lawyer, Prairie Schooner* 65 (Summer 1991): 131; Gary Davenport, review of *Indian Lawyer, Sewanee Review* 100 (Apr. 1992): 324.

18. Davenport 325.

19. James Welch, "Prologue," *Killing Custer* (New York: Penguin, 1995) 20.

20. Neil C. Mangum, review of *Killing Custer, Western Historical Quarterly* 26 (Winter 1995): 526.

21. Stella R. Swain, review of *Killing Custer, Journal of American Studies* 30 (Aug. 1996): 302; David N. Cremean, review of *Killing Custer, Western American Literature* 30 (Fall 1995): 301

22. James Welch, synopsis of *The Heartsong of Charging Elk,* personal correspondence, 12 Nov. 1998.

23. See William Bevis, "Native American Novels: Homing In," *Recovering the Word: Essays on Native American Literature,* ed. Brian Swann and Arnold Krupat (Berkeley: U of California P, 1987) 580–620.

24. Gish, "The Word Medicine of James Welch" 55.

25. William Bevis, "Wylie Tales: An Interview with James Welch," *Weber Studies* 12 (Fall 1995): 16.

26. O'Connell 62–63.

27. Wild 8.

28. Joseph Bruchac, "Contemporary Native American Writing: An Overview," *Handbook of Native American Literatures,* ed. Andrew Wiget (New York: Garland, 1996) 322.

29. Ibid., 323.

30. Ibid., 324.

31. Elizabeth Cook-Lynn, "American Indian Intellectualism and the New Indian Story," *American Indian Quarterly* 20 (Winter 1996): 71.

32. Ibid., 70.

33. Ibid., 67 and elsewhere.

34. Ibid., 74.

35. Ibid.

36. Ibid., 71–72.

37. O'Connell 68.

38. Bevis, "James Welch" 819.

39. O'Connell 65.

40. Ibid., 63; *see also* McFarland and Browning 8.

41. O'Connell 68.

42. Ibid., 70, 73.

43. Ibid., 70.

44. McFarland and Browning 18.

45. O'Connell 70.

46. McFarland and Browning 1.

47. Ibid., 2.

48. Ibid.

49. Alan R. Velie 67–90.

50. Wild 21

51. Ibid., 23.

52. Bevis, *Updating the Literary West* 23.

53. Richard White, review of *Fools Crow, New York Times Book Review* 30 Apr. 1995: 31.

54. O'Connell 63.

55. Bruchac, "Contemporary Native American Writing" 323.

56. Ibid., 324.

Chapter Two: *Riding the Earthboy 40*

1. Bill Bevis, "Dialogue with James Welch," *Northwest Review* 20 (1982): 184–85; *see also* McFarland and Browning 7.

2. William Matthews, "Introduction: Old Haunts," *The Real West Marginal Way: A Poet's Autobiography,* ed. Ripley S. Hugo, Lois Welch, and James Welch (New York: Norton, 1986) xvii.

3. Matthews xix.

4. Velie 71; *see also* Wild 14.

5. Kenneth Lincoln, "Blackfeet Winter Blues," *James Welch,* ed. McFarland, 99; excerpted from Lincoln, *Three American Literatures* (New York: Modern Language Association, 1982).

6. James Welch, *Riding the Earthboy 40,* rev. ed. (New York: Harper and Row, 1976) 51.

7. Velie, "Welch: Blackfeet Surrealism" 79.

8. Wild 17.

9. Velie 90.

10. Richard Hugo, "Stray Thoughts on Roethke and Teaching," *The Triggering Town: Lectures and Essays on Poetry and Writing* (New York: Norton, 1979) 27.

11. Ibid., 29.

12. Ibid., 29.

13. Cook-Lynn 72.

14. Robert Holland, review of *Riding the Earthboy 40, Poetry* 129 (Feb. 1977): 288.

15. Ibid., 289.

16. Jascha Kessler, review of *Riding the Earthboy 40, Saturday Review* 2 Oct. 1971: 50.

17. Andrew Wiget, *Native American Literature* (Boston: Twayne, 1985) 104.

18. Joseph Bruchac, "'I Just Kept My Eyes Open': An Interview

with James Welch," *Survival This Way: Interviews with American Indian Poets* (Tucson: Sun Tracks and U of Arizona P, 1987) 311.

19. Mark Jarman and David Mason, preface, *Rebel Angels: 25 Poets of the New Formalism* (Brownsville, OR: Story Line, 1996) xvi.

20. Paul Hoover, introduction, *Postmodern American Poetry* (New York: Norton, 1994) xxxv.

21. Peter Blue Cloud, *Clans of Many Nations: Selected Poems 1969–1994* (Fredonia, NY: White Pine, 1995) 75.

22. Duane Niatum, *Drawings of the Song Animals: New and Selected Poems* (Duluth: Holy Cow, 1991) 99.

23. John Bellante and Carl Bellante, "Sherman Alexie, Literary Rebel: An Excerpt from an Interview," *Bloomsbury Review* 14 (May–June 1994): 15.

24. Marnie Walsh, *A Taste of the Knife* (Boise, ID: Ahsahta, 1976) 2.

25. Sherman Alexie, *The Business of Fancydancing* (Brooklyn: Hanging Loose, 1992) 35.

26. Kathryn S. Vangen, "James Welch," *Handbook of Native American Literature,* ed. Wiget 532.

27. Elaine Jahner, "Quick Paces and a Space of Mind," *Denver Quarterly* 14 (Winter 1980): 37.

28. Ibid., 39.

29. Bevis, "Dialogue with James Welch" 181.

30. Vangen 533.

31. Ibid.

32. Velie 74.

33. Ibid., 75.

34. Vangen 533.

35. Bruchac, "I Just Kept My Eyes Open" 314.

36. Bevis, "James Welch" 809.

37. George Bird Grinnell, *Blackfoot Lodge Tales: The Story of a Prairie People* (Lincoln: U of Nebraska P, 1962) 113–16.

38. Robert Lowell, *"Life Studies" and "For the Union Dead"* (New York: Farrar, Straus and Giroux, 1967) 90.

39. Vangen 533.

40. Velie 87.

41. Wild 21.

42. Ibid., 22.

43. Lincoln, "Blackfeet Winter Blues" 104.

Chapter Three: *Winter in the Blood* as American Picaresque Classic

1. Stephen Tatum, "'Distance,' Desire, and the Ideological Matrix in *Winter in the Blood*," *Arizona Quarterly* 46 (Summer 1990): 87.

2. Jim Charles and Richard Predmore, "When Critical Approaches Converge: Team-Teaching Welch's *Winter in the Blood*," *Studies in American Indian Literature (SAIL)* 8 (Summer 1996): 49, 54.

3. Reynolds Price, review of *Winter in the Blood, New York Times Book Review* 10 Nov. 1974: 1.

4. Sale 20.

5. Ibid., 22.

6. Larson, review of *Winter in the Blood* 27.

7. Ibid., 26.

8. Review of *Winter in the Blood, New Yorker* 23 Dec. 1974: 84.

9. Margo Jefferson, review of *Winter in the Blood, Newsweek* 11 Nov. 1974: 119.

10. O'Connell 68.

11. Ibid., 73.

12. Ibid., 70.

13. Bevis, "Dialogue with James Welch" 164–65.

14. McFarland and Browning 2.

15. Bevis, "Dialogue with James Welch" 163.

16. Ibid., 163; *see also* O'Connell 71 and McFarland and Browning 18. William Kittredge's published work includes two collections of short fiction, numerous essays on environmental issues in the Northwest, and a powerful memoir, *Hole in the Sky,* which appeared in 1992.

17. O'Connell 71.

18. McFarland and Browning 18.

19. James Welch, *Winter in the Blood* (New York: Viking Penguin, 1986) 134.

20. O'Connell 69.

21. A. LaVonne Ruoff, "The Influence of Elio Vittorini's *In Sicily* on James Welch's *Winter in the Blood,*" *Native American Literatures,* ed. Laura Coltelli (Pisa: SEU, 1989) 143.

22. Joy Hambuechen Potter, *Elio Vittorini* (Boston: Twayne, 1979) 15.

23. Ernest Hemingway, "Introduction," *In Sicily* (New York: New Directions, 1949) 9.

24. Laura Coltelli, "James Welch," *Winged Words: American Indian Writers Speak* (Lincoln: U of Nebraska P, 1990) 198. Interview conducted 12 Sept. 1985.

25. Elio Vittorini, *In Sicily* (New York: New Directions, 1949) 13.

26. "The Only Good Indian, Section I of a Novel in Progress," editorial, *South Dakota Review* 9 (Summer 1971) 54.

27. Coltelli 193.

28. Ibid., 194.

29. Ibid., 188.

30. Bevis "Native American Novels" 587.

31. "The Only Good Indian" 54.

32. Bevis, "Dialogue with James Welch" 166.

33. Ibid.

34. Ibid., 166–67.

35. Ibid., 167.

36. O'Connell 69.

37. Ibid.,

38. Ibid., 71.

39. A. LaVonne Ruoff, "Alienation and the Female Principle in *Winter in the Blood*," *James Welch,* ed. McFarland 76. Reprinted with revisions from *American Indian Quarterly* 4 (May 1978): 107–21. The Confluence Press reprint includes Ruoff's "History in *Winter in the Blood*" from *American Indian Quarterly* as an addition to the endnotes of the essay above.

40. Peter G. Beidler and A. LaVonne Ruoff, "A Discussion of *Winter in the Blood*," *American Indian Quarterly* 4 (May 1978): 160. From an edited transcript of discussions at the symposium on the novel held at the Modern Language Association convention in Chicago on 30 Dec. 1977. Papers from that session form the foundation of this "Special Symposium Issue" on *Winter in the Blood.*

41. Coltelli 186, 187.

42. Nora Baker Barry, "*Winter in the Blood* as Elegy," *American Indian Quarterly* 4 (May 1978): 156.

43. Beidler and Ruoff 167.

44. Ibid., 163.

45. Tatum 95, 96.

46. Bevis, "Dialogue with James Welch" 165.

47. Robert Alter, *Rogue's Progress: Studies in the Picaresque Novel* (Cambridge: Harvard UP, 1964) viii.

48. Alexander A. Parker, *Literature and the Delinquent: The Picaresque Novel in Spain and Europe 1599–1753* (Edinburgh: U of Edinburgh P, 1967) 20.

49. Stuart Miller, *The Picaresque Novel* (Cleveland, OH: Case Western Reserve UP, 1967) 10.

50. Ibid., 12.

51. Parker 4.

52. Miller 86.

53. Ibid., 47.

54. Ibid., 49.

55. Ibid., 30.

56. Peter G. Beidler, "Preface: A Special Symposium Issue," *American Indian Quarterly* 4 (May 1978): 93.

57. Ibid., 94.

58. Ibid., 95.

59. Kathleen Sands, "Alienation and Broken Narrative in *Winter in the Blood,*" *American Indian Quarterly* 4 (May 1978): 97; reprinted in *Critical Essays on Native American literature,* ed. Andrew Wiget (Boston: G.K. Hall, 1985) 230–38.

60. John Scheckter, "James Welch: Settling Up on the Reservation," *South Dakota Review* 24 (Summer 1986): 12.

61. Cook-Lynn 69.

62. Paul Eisenstein, "Finding Lost Generations: Recovering Omitted History in *Winter in the Blood,*" *Multi-Ethnic Literatures of the United States (MELUS)* 19 (Fall 1995): 10.

63. Eisenstein 15.

64. John Purdy, "'He Was Going Along': Motion in the Novels of James Welch," *American Indian Quarterly* 14 (Spring 1990): 144.

65. William W. Thackery, "'Crying for Pity' in *Winter in the Blood,*" *MELUS* 7 (Spring 1980): 61–78; "Animal Allies and Transformers of *Winter in the Blood,*" *MELUS* 12 (Spring 1985): 37–64.

66. *See* n. 40.

67. Paula Gunn Allen, "Stranger in My Own Life: Alienation in Indian Literature," *MELUS* 7 (Summer 1980): 4.

68. Arnold Krupat, "Critical Approaches to Native American Literature," *Handbook of Native American Literature,* ed. Wiget 329.

69. Allen, "Stranger in My Own Life" 15.

70. Alan R. Velie, "Indians in Indian Fiction: The Shadow of the Trickster," *American Indian Quarterly* 8 (Fall 1984): 317.

71. Allen, "Stranger in My Own Life" 18.

72. Velie, "Indians in Indian Fiction" 315.

73. Allen, "Stranger in My Own Life" 18.

74. McFarland and Browning 9.

75. Andrew Horton, "The Bitter Humor of *Winter in the Blood,*" *American Indian Quarterly* 4 (May 1978): 131.

76. Ibid., 132.

77. Ibid., 138.

78. Barry, "*Winter in the Blood* as Elegy" 156.

79. Alan R. Velie, *Four American Indian Literary Masters,* 92, 95.

80. Velie, "Indians in Indian Fiction" 319.

81. Charles G. Ballard, "The Theme of the Helping Hand in *Winter in the Blood,*" *MELUS* 17 (Spring 1991–92): 68.

82. Kenneth Lincoln, *Ind'n Humor* (New York: Oxford UP, 1993) 254.

83. Ibid., 268.

84. Ibid., 272, 273.

85. Larson, *American Indian Fiction* 148.

86. Lincoln, *Ind'n Humor* 274.

87. Gish, "The Word Medicine of James Welch" 56.

88. Ballard 68.

89. Wild 36–37.

90. Charles and Predmore 47.

91. Louis Owens, "Earthboy's Return: James Welch's Acts of Recovery," *Other Destinies: Understanding the American Indian Novel* (Norman: U of Oklahoma P, 1992): 128–66.

92. Jack L. Davis, "Restoration of Indian Identity in *Winter in the Blood,*" in *James Welch,* Ron McFarland, ed. (Lewiston, ID: Confluence, 1986) 42.

Chapter Four: The Tragedy of Jim Loney

1. Bevis, "James Welch" 813.

2. Anatole Broyard, review of *The Death of Jim Loney, New York Times* 28 Nov. 1979: C25.

3. Andrew Wiget, review of *The Death of Jim Loney, Choice* June 1986: 1508; Bevis, "James Welch" 813.

4. C. M. Klein, review of *The Death of Jim Loney, Library Journal* 1 Sept. 1979: 1722.

5. Sands, *"The Death of Jim Loney:* Indian or Not?" 127.

6. Wild 41.

7. Ibid., 45.

8. Vangen 535.

9. Frederick Turner, review of *The Death of Jim Loney, Nation* 24 Nov. 1979: 538.

10. Paul N. Pavich, review of *The Death of Jim Loney, Western American Literature* 15 (Fall 1980): 220.

11. Bevis, "Native American Novels" 617.

12. Sands, *"The Death of Jim Loney:* Indian or Not?" 127, 132.

13. Kenneth Lincoln, review of *The Death of Jim Loney, American Indian Culture and Research Journal* 4 (1980): 179; Roberta Orlandini, "Variations on a Theme: Traditions and Temporal Structure in the Novels of James Welch," *South Dakota Review* 26 (Autumn 1988): 43; Owens, "Earthboy's Return" 147.

14. Wild 43.

15. Robert M. Nelson, *Place and Vision: The Function of Landscape in Native American Fiction* (New York: Peter Lang, 1993) 94. This forty-page chapter focuses on the role of landscape as a "cure for the disease of alienation" (131), which "*is* the human condition" in an existential universe (96).

16. Ibid., 104.

17. James Welch, *The Death of Jim Loney* (New York: Harper and Row, 1979) 4.

18. Wiget, *Native American Literature* 93.

19. Gish, "The Word Medicine of James Welch" 68.

20. Bevis, "James Welch" 817.

21. Owens, "Earthboy's Return" 153.

22. Ibid., 154.

23. Patricia Riley In-the Woods, *"The Death of Jim Loney:* A Ritual of Re-Creation," *Fiction International* 20 (1991): 164–65.

24. Nora Barry, "'The Lost Children' in James Welch's *The Death of Jim Loney,*" *Western American Literature* 25 (May 1990): 42.

25. Nelson 127.

26. Paula Gunn Allen, *The Sacred Hoop: Recovering the Feminine in American Indian Traditions* (Boston: Beacon, 1986) 145.

27. Bevis, "Dialogue with James Welch" 176.

28. McFarland and Browning 10, 11.

29. Ibid., 10.

30. Wild 43.

31. Gish, "The Word Medicine of James Welch" 68, 69.

32. Dexter Westrum, "The Way the Bird Works in *The Death of Jim Loney." James Welch,* ed. McFarland 145.

33. Owens, "Earthboy's Return" 155.

34. Allen, *The Sacred Hoop* 93.

35. Sands, *"The Death of Jim Loney:* Indian or Not?" 131.

36. David M. Craig, "Beyond Assimilation: James Welch and the Indian Dilemma," *North Dakota Quarterly* 53 (Spring 1985): 188.

37. Scheckter 16.

38. Barry, "The Lost Children" 35.

39. John Purdy, *"Bha's* and *The Death of Jim Loney," SAIL* 5 (Summer 1993): 70.

40. Craig 184.

41. Nelson 127.

42. Rachel Barritt Costa, "Incommunicability: A Linguistic Analysis of Conversation Breakdown in *The Death of Jim Loney,*" *Native American Literatures,* ed. Coltelli 159.

43. Lincoln, *Ind'n Humor* 254.

44. Wiget, *Native American Literature* 93–94.

45. Ronald E. McFarland, "Women's Roles in Contemporary Native American Writing and in Welch's *The Death of Jim Loney,*" *James Welch,* ed. McFarland 153, 154.

46. Judith A. Antell, "Momaday, Welch, and Silko: Expressing the Feminine Principle through Male Alienation," *American Indian Quarterly* 12 (Summer 1988): 216.

47. Wild 41; Allen, 145.

Chapter Five: The Epic Design of *Fools Crow*

1. Bruchac, "I Just Kept My Eyes Open" 321.

2. Purdy, "He Was Going Along" 135.

3. Gish, "The Word Medicine of James Welch" 71.

4. James Welch, *Fools Crow* (New York: Viking Penguin, 1986) 15.

5. Bevis, "James Welch" 819–20.

6. Ernest Hemingway, *For Whom the Bell Tolls* (New York: Scribner's, 1940) 66.

7. Gish, "The Word Medicine of James Welch" 71.

8. Bevis, "James Welch" 820.

9. Owens, "Earthboy's Return" 158.

10. Ibid., 162.

11. Ibid., 159.

12. Grinnell 222.

13. McFarland and Browning 5.

14. Bevis, "James Welch" 823.

15. Owens, "Earthboy's Return" 161; *see also* Orlandini, "Variations on a Theme" 48.

16. Purdy, "He Was Going Along" 138.

17. Ibid.,

18. Gish, "The Word Medicine of James Welch" 72–73, 76.

19. John C. Ewers, *The Blackfeet: Raiders on the Northwestern Plains* (Norman: U of Oklahoma P, 1958) 250.

20. Gish, "The Word Medicine of James Welch" 73.

21. Owens, "Earthboy's Return"165.

22. Ron McFarland, "'The End' in James Welch's Novels," *American Indian Quarterly* 17 (Summer 1993): 324.

23. Bevis, "James Welch" 820.

24. Nora Barry, "'A Myth to Be Alive': James Welch's *Fools Crow*," *MELUS* 17 (Spring 1991–92): 17.

Chapter Six: Going One-on-One

1. James Welch, *The Indian Lawyer* (New York: Norton, 1990) 303, 327.

2. J. W. Parins, review of *The Indian Lawyer, Choice* 28 (Mar. 1991): 1139; Walter Walker, review of *The Indian Lawyer, Washington Post Book World* 12 Dec. 1990: 9.

3. David Seals, review of *The Indian Lawyer, Nation* 251 (26 Nov. 1990): 649.

4. Seals 650.

5. Lemon 131.

6. E. Hoagland 7; W. Hoagland 257.

7. Sale 21.

8. Sidner J. Larson, "The Outsider in James Welch's *The Indian Lawyer*," *American Indian Quarterly* 18 (Fall 1994): 505.

9. Alan R. Velie, "American Indian Literature in the Nineties: The Emergence of the Middle-Class Protagonist," *World Literature Today* 66 (Spring 1992): 265.

10. S. Larson 502.

11. Ibid., 503.

12. Peter Donahue, "New Warriors, New Legends: Basketball in Three Native American Works of Fiction," *American Indian Culture and Research Journal* 21.2 (1997): 49, 50.

13. Bevis, "James Welch" 824.

14. An essay by Robert Gish, "Mystery and Mock Intrigue in James Welch's *Winter in the Blood,*" suggests Welch's interest in that kind of plot. *See* Ron McFarland, *James Welch* (Lewiston, ID: Confluence Press, 1986) 45–57; reprinted in Gish, *Beyond Bounds: Cross-Cultural Essays on Anglo, American Indians, and Chicano Literature* (Albuquerque: University of New Mexico Press, 1996). Although Gish observes in his more recent commentary that Welch offers the reader "an especially intriguing plot and 'hero'" (83) in *The Indian Lawyer,* he does not comment on it specifically as a novel of intrigue.

15. Gish, *Beyond Bounds* 79; S. Larson 504.

16. Gish, *Beyond Bounds* 85.

17. S. Larson 505.

18. Ibid., 504.

19. Bevis, "Native American Novels" 580–619.

20. Bevis, "James Welch" 824.

21. Cook-Lynn 71, 69.

22. Davenport 324, 325.

Chapter Seven: Custer as Native American Text

1. Bevis, "Wylie Tales" 16–17.

2. James Welch, with Peter Stekler, *Killing Custer: The Battle of the Little Bighorn and the Fate of the Plains Indians* (New York: Norton, 1994) 20.

3. Welch, *The Death of Jim Loney* 50.

4. Welch, *The Indian Lawyer* 219.

5. Mangum 526.

6. Richard White, review of *Killing Custer, New York Times Book Review* 30 Apr. 1995: 31.

7. Cremean 301.

8. Ibid., 302.

9. White 31.

10. Helen Carr, review of *Killing Custer, New Statesman* 31 Mar. 1995: 39.

11. Dennis Held, manuscript of "An Interview with James Welch," *Writer's NW* 8 (Spring 1993): 1–2. This passage is among those excluded from the published version of the interview.

12. Ibid.,

13. Ibid.,

14. Ibid.

15. Bevis, "Wylie Tales" 27.

16. Policies have probably changed at the battlefield site since 1974. For the record, the Bear Paw Battlefield, which is a national historical park in northern Montana and which marks the spot where more than 150 Nez Perces were killed in combat with elements of the 7th Cavalry, among other units, is equipped with sheltered picnic tables.

17. O'Connell 70.

18. Bevis, "Wylie Tales"16.

19. Ibid., 27.

20. Held 2.

Conclusion

1. Dexter Westrum, "James Welch's *Fools Crow:* Back to the Future," *San Jose Studies* 14 (Spring 1988): 50.

2. Ibid.,

3. Ibid., 57.

4. James Welch, synopsis of *The Heartsong of Charging Elk*, personal correspondence, 1 Nov. 1998.

5. John C. Neihardt, *Black Elk Speaks* (New York: Washington Square, 1972) 181–94.

6. S. Larson 505.

ANNOTATED BIBLIOGRAPHY

Compiled by Ron McFarland and James Mayo

James Welch's manuscripts are in the archives of the Beinecke Rare Book Library at Yale University.

I. Books by James Welch

Fiction

Winter in the Blood. New York: Harper and Row, 1974.
The Death of Jim Loney. New York: Harper and Row, 1979.
Fools Crow. New York: Viking, 1986.
Indian Lawyer. New York: Norton, 1990.

Poetry

Riding the Earthboy 40. New York: World, 1971; revised edition, New York: Harper and Row, 1976.

Nonfiction

Killing Custer. With Paul K. Stekler. New York: Norton, 1994.

II. Bibliography

Colonnese, Tom, and Louis Owens. "James Welch." *American Indian Novelists: An Annotated Critical Bibliography.* New York: Garland, 1985. 131–54. Covers the first two novels and the poems, including periodical publication, annotates thirty-two critical commentaries, and lists book reviews of the novels.

III. Special Journal Issue on James Welch

Beidler, Peter G. Special Symposium Issue on James Welch's *Winter in the Blood. American Indian Quarterly* 4 (May 1978). Collects six essays from the seminar held at the Modern Language Association convention in 1977 along with two additional commentaries and a preface: Kathleen M. Sands, "Alienation and Broken Narrative in *Winter in the Blood*"; A. LaVonne Ruoff, "Alienation and the Female Principle in *Winter in the Blood*"; Louise K. Barnett, "Alienation and Ritual in *Winter in the Blood*"; Andrew Horton, "The Bitter Humor of *Winter in the Blood*"; Alan R. Velie, "*Winter in the Blood* as Comic Novel"; Nora Baker Berry, "*Winter in the Blood* as Elegy"; Beidler and Ruoff, editors, "A Discussion of *Winter in the Blood*"; Ruoff, "History in *Winter in the Blood:* Backgrounds and Bibliography."

IV. Books and Pamphlets on James Welch

McFarland, Ron. *James Welch.* Lewiston, ID: Confluence, 1986. Presents selections from *Winter in the Blood, Riding the Earthboy 40, The Death of Jim Loney,* and *Fools Crow* (then an untitled novel in progress) along with reprints of A. LaVonne Ruoff's essays from the symposium issue of *American Indian Quarterly* (see above), Kenneth Lincoln's "Blackfeet Winter Blues," from *Three American Literatures,* and Kathleen Sands's "*The Death of Jim Loney:* Indian or Not?" from *SAIL,* along with seven new essays: Jack L. Davis, "Restoration of Indian Identity in *Winter in the Blood*"; Robert Gish, "Mystery and Mock Intrigue in James Welch's *Winter in the Blood*"; Peter Wild, "Almost Not on the Map" (on the poems); Kim Stafford, "At the Only Bar in Dixon" (on the poems); William Thackery, "The Dance of Jim Loney"; Dexter Westrum, "Transcendental Survival: The Way the Bird Works in *The Death of Jim Loney*"; Ronald E. McFarland, "Women's Roles in Contemporary Native American Writing and in Welch's *The Death of Jim Loney*." Also includes an interview with Welch, a chronology, and a bibliography accompanied by lengthy errata.

Wild, Peter. *James Welch.* Western Writers Series 57. Boise: Boise State UP, 1983. Includes commentary on the poems, appreciation of *Winter in the Blood,* and a brief, unsympathetic glance at *The Death of Jim Loney.*

V. Selected Interviews

Bevis, Bill. "Dialogue with James Welch." *Northwest Review* 20 (1982): 163–85.

———. "Wylie Tales: An Interview with James Welch," *Weber Studies* 12 (Fall 1995): 15–31.

Bruchac, Joseph. "'I Just Kept My Eyes Open': An Interview with James Welch." *Survival This Way: Interviews with American Indian Poets.* Tucson: Sun Tracks and U of Arizona P, 1987. 311–21.

Coltelli, Linda. "James Welch." *Winged Words: American Indian Writers Speak.* Lincoln: U of Nebraska P, 1990. 185–99.

Held, Dennis. "An Interview with James Welch." *Writer's NW* 8 (Spring 1993): 1–2.

O'Connell, Nicholas. "James Welch." *At the Field's End: Interviews with 20 Pacific Northwest Writers.* Seattle: Madrona, 1987. 58–75.

VI. Books with Chapters on James Welch

Berner, Robert L. "Quaternity in James Welch's *Fools Crow*." *Entering the 90s: The North American Experience.* Ed. Thomas E. Schirer. Sault Ste. Marie, MI: Lake Superior State UP, 1991. 108–13. Applies symbolic values of the four directions as defined in *Black Elk Speaks* to Welch's novel.

ANNOTATED BIBLIOGRAPHY

Bevis, William. "Native American Novels: Homing In." *Recovering the Word: Essays on Native American Literature*. Ed. Brian Swann and Arnold Krupat. Berkeley: U of California P, 1987. 580–620. Contrasts tribal "homing" to white competitive individualism in several Native American novels, with special emphasis on *The Death of Jim Loney*.

———. "James Welch." *Updating the Literary West*. Western Literature Association. Fort Worth: Texas Christian UP, 1997. 808–826. Surveys the work through *Killing Custer* with slight attention to the poems and the two most recent books; focuses on *The Death of Jim Loney* as a novel on "the mixed-blood's situation" and on *Fools Crow* as an "epic novel" and "the documentation of an entire culture."

Gish, Robert. "The Word Medicine of James Welch." *Beyond Bounds: Cross-Cultural Essays on Anglo, Indian and Chicano Literature*. Albuquerque: U of New Mexico P, 1996. 54–85. Comments on the four novels, drawing the section on "mystery and mock intrigue" in *Winter in the Blood* from an earlier essay, describing *Fools Crow* as exemplary of "the word as medicine," and contrasting *The Indian Lawyer* to the "commercial slickness" of Kevin Costner's movie *Dances with Wolves*.

Larson, Charles R. "Winter in the Blood." *American Indian Fiction*. Albuquerque: U of New Mexico P, 1978. 140–49. Calls it "an almost flawless novel" and admires the "general feeling of goodwill" and depiction of the reservation as "a place of warmth and fulfillment, where the survivors of today find a life-affirming sense of belonging."

Lincoln, Kenneth. "Red Gods, Blue Humors: James Welch." *Ind'n Humor*. New York: Oxford UP, 1993: 254–79. Examines the "dark" and "desacralized" humor of *Winter in the Blood* as "an absurdist cry of survival."

———. "Blackfeet Winter Blues." *Native American Renaissance*. Berkeley: U of California P, 1983. 148–82. Comments on the role of

ANNOTATED BIBLIOGRAPHY

Na'pi (Old Man, a trickster) in *Winter in the Blood* and on the operation of a "Blackfeet epistemology" therein, but finds little evidence of "older ethnology" in *The Death of Jim Loney;* also comments on the poems.

Nelson, Robert M. "The Function of the Landscape of *The Death of Jim Loney.*" *Place and Vision: The Function of Landscape in Native American Fiction.* New York: Peter Lang, 1993. 91–131. Points out elements in the landscape of the Montana Highline that lead Loney toward "complete reintegration of his life with the regenerative spirit of the land" and "a cure for the disease of alienation."

Owens, Louis. "Earthboy's Return: James Welch's Acts of Recovery." *Other Destinies: Understanding the American Indian Novel.* Norman: U of Oklahoma P, 1992. 128–66. About half of the chapter concerns *Winter in the Blood* and none of it deals with *The Indian Lawyer;* sees Jim Loney as victim of "the authoritative discourse" that defines what it is to be Indian; presents *Fools Crow* as the counter to *The Death of Jim Loney* and as "the most profound act of recovery in American literature."

Scheckter, John. "Now That the (Water) Buffalo's Gone: James Welch and the Transcultural Novel." *Entering the 90s: The North American Experience.* Ed. Thomas E. Schirer. Sault Ste. Marie, MI: Lake Superior State UP, 1991. 101–7. Reads *Fools Crow* in light of other postcolonial novels (Rushdie's *The Satanic Verses,* Maalouf's *Leo Africanus,* Colin Johnson's *Doctor Wooredy's Prescription for Enduring the Ending of the World*).

Vangen, Kathryn S. "James Welch." *Handbook of Native American Literature.* Ed. Andrew Wiget. New York: Garland, 1996. 531–37. Briefly surveys the poems and the first three novels, detecting in all of Welch's work a "ritual of exorcism."

Velie, Alan R. "Welch: Blackfoot Surrealism" and "*Winter in the Blood:* Welch and the Comic Novel." *Four American Indian Liter-*

ary Masters. Norman: U of Oklahoma P, 1982. 66–90, 91–103. Defines the term "surrealism" and traces it via Peruvian poet Cesar Vallejo and James Wright to Welch; examines ten of the poems rather closely. Regards *Winter in the Blood* as "a masterpiece of comic fiction" varying from "raucous farce to subtle satire," with most of the humor being verbal.

VII. Critical Articles on James Welch

Allen, Paula Gunn. "A Stranger in My Own Life: Alienation in American Indian Prose and Poetry." *MELUS* 7 (Summer 1980): 3–19. Focuses on the protagonists' cultural alienation in several Indian novels, including *Winter in the Blood* and *The Death of Jim Loney;* sees Loney's death as a matter of choice, to die like a warrior.

Ballard, Charles. "The Question of Survival in *Fools Crow.*" *North Dakota Quarterly* 59 (Fall 1991): 251–59. Treats *Fools Crow* as an epic novel and suggests that the survivor may be neither the title character nor his renegade friend Fast Horse, but the mythic idea of the culture embodied in the visionary So-at-sa-ki, Feather Woman.

Barry, Nora. "'The Lost Children' in James Welch's *The Death of Jim Loney.*" *Western American Literature* 25 (May 1990): 35–48. Connects the novel with Gros Ventre and Blackfeet myths of abandoned children.

———. "'A Myth to Be Alive': James Welch's *Fools Crow.*" *MELUS* 17 (Spring 1991–92): 3–20. Discusses Fools Crow's role as culture hero and his relationship with the Scarface myth, connected with the Sun Dance ritual.

Craig, David M. "Beyond Assimilation: James Welch and the Indian Dilemma." *North Dakota Quarterly* 53 (Spring 1985): 182–90.

Suggests a three-part "shape" for the first two novels: estrangement, search for self (identity), return to the Indian world, the dilemma being not assimilation but survival.

Eisenstein, Paul. "Finding Lost Generations: Recovering Omitted History in *Winter in the Blood.*" *MELUS* 19 (Fall 1994): 3–18. Reflects on Hemingway's influence, including his doctrine of omission and the need of the speaker in the novel for omitted or repressed history.

Gish, Robert. F. "New Warrior, New West: History and Advocacy in James Welch's *The Indian Lawyer.*" *American Indian Quarterly* 15 (Summer 1991): 369–74. Comments on shift of emphasis from bucolic, rural West of yore to issues of post-frontier, urban West of the twentieth century and argues that Sylvester Yellow Calf will run for Congress again as a result of his return to home and tribal heritage.

Goble, Ron. "Sovereignty in the Blood: Cultural Resistance in the Characters of James Welch." *Wicazo Sa Review* 9 (Fall 1993): 37–43. Suggests that *Fools Crow* and *Indian Lawyer* embody the extremes of tribal sovereignty, with the other two novels exemplifying "reaffirmation of tribal sovereignty" between those extremes.

Jahner, Elaine. "Quick Paces and a Space of Mind." *Denver Quarterly* 14 (Winter 1980): 34–47. Focuses on the theme of distance in both the poems and *Winter in the Blood.*

Kunz, Don. "Lost in the Distance of Winter: James Welch's *Winter in the Blood.*" *Critique* 20.1 (1978): 93–99. Indicates use of physical, emotional, and aesthetic distance in the novel.

Larson, Sidner J. "The Outsider in James Welch's *The Indian Lawyer.*" *American Indian Quarterly* 18 (Fall 1994): 495–506. Focuses on identity theme with particular attention to the impact of women on the protagonist.

ANNOTATED BIBLIOGRAPHY

McClure, A. B. "A Literary Criticism: Mixed Blood Reading." *Wica-zo Sa Review* 10 (Fall 1995): 79–83. Argues that contrast between Loney and his sister "vindicates him as a Native American"; detects some positive aspect to his death.

McFarland, Ron. "'The End' in James Welch's Novels." *American Indian Quarterly* 17 (Summer 1993): 319–27. Reflects on the element of uncertainty or ambiguity in the conclusions to Welch's four novels.

Orlandini, Roberta. "Variations on a Theme: Tradition and Temporal Structure in the Novels of James Welch." *South Dakota Review* 26 (Autumn 1988): 37–52. Examines function of ethnic traditions in the first three novels, particularly the value of dreams and visions for Fools Crow, who suffers less from cultural conflict and detachment from heritage than the two earlier protagonists.

Purdy, John. "'He Was Going Along': Motion in the Novels of James Welch." *American Indian Quarterly* 14 (Spring 1990): 133–45. Deals with journeys and movement, particularly as they concern the search for individual or communal identity in *Fools Crow*.

Riley In-The-Woods, Patricia. "*The Death of Jim Loney:* A Ritual of Re-Creation." *Fiction International* 20 (1991): 157–66. Connects events in the novel with sacrificial re-creation ritual of the "earth diver" in Blackfeet mythology.

Sands, Kathleen. "Closing the Distance: Critic, Reader and the Works of James Welch." *MELUS* 14 (Summer 1987): 73–85. Prevailing tone of "sadness" in Welch's poems and novels reflects "survival in spite of loss"; novels grow out of the "spareness" of the poems and of the landscape itself; concludes it is the land that "makes the distance bearable."

Scheckter, John. "James Welch: Settling Up on the Reservation." *South Dakota Review* 24 (Summer 1986): 7–19. Argues that the first two novels depict characters who are haunted by cultural myth and history that bring little consolation, which makes the maintenance of a sense of "individual dignity" and personal integrity an "absolute necessity."

Smith, William F., Jr. "*Winter in the Blood:* The Indian Cowboy as Everyman." *Michigan Academician* 2 (Fall 1977): 299–306. Traces influence of detective fiction and Westerns on the novel.

Tardieu, Betty. "Communion in James Welch's *Winter in the Blood.*" *SAIL* 5 (Winter 1993): 69. Examines blending of Christian and Native American rituals in the novel and argues that Christian Communion unites body and spirit and breaks the linear mold, moving it closer to a Native American perspective.

Tatum, Stephen. "'Distance,' Desire, and the Ideological Matrix of *Winter in the Blood.*" *Arizona Quarterly* 46 (Summer 1990): 73–100. Examines "how the paradox of desire locates larger textual disorders of both form and meaning"; informed by recent developments in and jargon of current critical theory.

Thackery, William W. "Animal Allies and Transformations of *Winter in the Blood*" MELUS 12 (Spring 1985): 37–64. Provides sources from Blackfeet and Gros Ventre mythology for understanding Welch's use of animals in the novel.

———. "'Crying for Pity' in *Winter in the Blood.*" *MELUS* 7 (Spring 1980): 61–78. Describes the narrator's progress toward visionary insight into himself as it pertains to the Gros Ventre initiation ceremony.

Velie, Alan R. "Indians in Indian Fiction: The Shadow of the Trickster." *American Indian Quarterly* 8 (Fall 1984): 315–29. Considers Momaday's *House Made of Dawn* along with Welch's first two novels, arguing for the figure of the trickster in all three of the protagonists (the Blackfeet Napi in Welch's case) in favor of the stereotype of the Indian as loser.

ANNOTATED BIBLIOGRAPHY

Westrum, Dexter. "James Welch's *Fools Crow:* Back to the Future." *San Jose Studies* 14 (Spring 1988): 49–58. Describes Fools Crow as the "spiritual archetype" of Welch's contemporary protagonists; suggests Raven as counterpart to Jim Loney's "dark bird."

INDEX